Hippo*

The Human Focused Digital Book

Pete Trainor

* The Hippocampus (named after its resemblance to the seahorse, from the Greek ἱππόκαμπος, "seahorse" from ἵππος hippos, "horse" and κάμπος kampos, "sea monster") is a major component of the brains of humans. The hippocampus belongs to the limbic system and plays important roles in the consolidation of information from short-term memory to long-term memory, and in spatial navigation.

Copyright © 2018 P.Trainor

Paperback ISBN 978-0-9955361-3-5
E-Book ISBN 978-0-9955361-2-8

Originally published in Great Britain in 2016 by Nexus CX Ltd

Hippo – The Human Focused Digital Book

Cover Art by Jamie Twyman
Edited by Luke Shipman

To my beautiful wife Merry, and my amazing kids Charlie and Phoebe – thank you for bringing out the very **best** human in me, every day.

Hippo – The Human Focused Digital Book

CONTENTS

Hippo – The Human Focused Digital Book

INTRODUCTION: THE ACCIDENTAL POLYMATH

'He who has a why to live can bear almost any how.' Friedrich Nietzsche

We don't create, we discover. Mostly we discover what is already there, by aligning ourselves to a position so that creations emerge. Aligning in order to bring things into material form. To bring them into—*manifestation.*

⌘

Hello there. It's Pete. If you're reading this on a screen, welcome to the digital era. If you're holding a paper book in your hands, I salute you. Very retro. Whatever your chosen platform is, it's okay. Everything is always *okay*—as we'll soon explore. This book is going to twist and turn, and you'll need to use a lot of your senses to process things, and understand what I'm trying to say and this is a good thing—to be tested. I want you to feel the polymath in you and embrace it.

You see, throughout history, it has been the polymaths who were capable of nurturing human progress, and this is a book about that – human progress – both historical and future progress. Da Vinci was a polymath who understood the necessity to study broadly and not locally and that in mastering an area or field that may appear disconnected to one's main sphere, we can, in fact, develop further knowledge within the main. His message was not only to study the science of art but also – the art of science. So I will begin with you holistically, and we won't avoid any area of thought that will contribute to the discussion of emergent technologies and the trajectory of innovation from now and out into future times. There are ways to help coordinate these growth patterns forward to develop the master within us, and that's what this book is: a set of thoughts to help co-ordinate us forward and to help improve the thinking needed to do so.

It may seem obvious but the apparatus we are born with to read a book like this and to appreciate the wonders are everything we need as tools to evolve. They are all that we need and nothing more. Empiricism emphasises this, and that the role of evidence drawn through the senses is the thing to form knowledge: advocating that the senses are *themselves* the holy grails we search for through our ideologies. In science and indeed, scripture, yes – the answers are all inbuilt, we just need to learn how to switch on the nose, ears, eyes, fingers and the tongue, and once the switches are active, the live brain can receive more information because we are then – plugged in – to the universe. That's what design is or at least should be: the bridge between us and our senses. Da Vinci was a genius, who taught that we could all stretch our intelligence to become like him and to achieve this flowering, we must develop these senses, stretch them and test them. This progressive method does not support a conforming or even satisfied inner spirit that is ever content, but one with a thirst for more knowledge. Thus, with the more holistic knowledge we have, the more points of reference we have, which will build the platform for more understanding.

During my time in the design and technology industry, a quiet revolution upended our concept of the way patterns work within our lives, societies, and organisations. From London to Laos, Mumbai to Manchester, Nunavut to Nairobi, digital tech has crept into our lives as if through stealth and so deeply has it penetrated us, that it has wholly redesigned life. Some say it is re-designing us. Hill stations in Nepal's Himalaya, desert posts in Africa's savannahs, in the deep oceans and the high skies, digital technology is now elemental in our landscape, and WiFi—as much a part of the ether as the wind and falling rain. It's not going to stop. From bricks and mortar tech, through to analogue, digital and into the beyond: we are about to observe more change in the next ten years, than of the last hundred. We have a lot of reasons to be excited about progress, yet some of the most popular trends—the proliferation of apps, the rise of the *sharing economy*, and the ubiquity of on-demand services—have not only brought about a greater degree of personalisation, convenience and economic growth, but also questions around what kind of life we want to live in the 21st century.

There's nothing normal about this current age of technological progress. When we can design so liberally and innovate so quickly, do we risk losing sight of our human purpose?

Take this as an example… the time it took to reach **50 million** people;

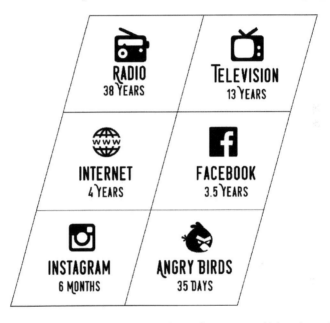

Extraordinary. Breathtaking in a lot of ways, terrifying in others, because we *built* that. We designed that change. If we applied the same design methodologies to some of the worlds big humanitarian and aid issues, who knows what we could achieve.

Before we go shooting off into the future of design, let's go right back to the very start. My start. School. I was never an academic; I knew that one early. In school, I was middle-tier in terms of how 'intelligence' was measured… *but there are many forms of intelligence.* 'Middle-tier' was just a smarter word for average but average based on—what? The group who were all being measured and tested on what was considered intelligent? We can all access the higher elements and culture our genius but to do this, we need to accept that the way this has been nurtured thus far has been somewhat 'mediated.' In no time, certain children are smart and others – not so much. Often these non-smart kids go on to build bridges, create great artworks and write best-selling novels. Not so smart? Or misunderstood? Perhaps the measuring tools to decide who and what is intelligent are all out of whack to begin with.

It was 1996, and I left school with few transferable skills or qualifications As far as education was concerned, I had no desire for any more of it; it had served its purpose. I found myself working in one of the most pervasive industries of the last twenty years... digital design. Was it a chance happening... or fate? With this one... I am still *discovering*. I was thrown a lifeline and handed a job in the computer-based training department of a helicopter manufacturer, of all places. Grafting at the dirty jobs no one else wanted. It was an apprenticeship in design that made me feel like I was somebody.

I've since discovered that there are only four stages of learning:

1. Unconsciously-incapable (the most fun)
2. Consciously-incapable
3. Consciously-capable
4. Unconsciously-capable

I was at stage 1. You know – when we experience going for new things with no handle on how we are doing them wrong. It was playtime again – I was in a room full of computers and it was the best time of my life. Kicking back with the designers and programmers who were older and all 'graduated'. I was in my new element and you know that thing when you don't realise you're happy when you are? That was me, right there – working with hackers, makers, coders and pirates.

Two years into my design apprenticeship I was approached to leave and join another company called *Third Dimension*. We where building virtual reality worlds and simulators. Again, I had no idea this was the frontier. I was wet behind the ears, gullible, I could be led anywhere and I got lucky. My role with Third Dimension naturally evolved with the times and we began to create something called 'websites' for this thing called 'the Internet'. I found myself in a world of "HCI" – Human-Computer Interaction. I was unwittingly at the forefront of a movement, riding a beautiful wave, one that would change the sea current forever... and I had no idea! All things had converged, self-arranged, 'aligned' and things were taking form – they were manifesting.

It wasn't long after I started working with Third Dimension that I read futurist Ray Kurzweil seminal work, *The Age Of Spiritual Machines*. In it, Kurzweil predicted a new era of thinking machines that will exceed human intelligence. But what type of intelligence? The idea seemed outlandish… but exciting nonetheless. Back in the 90s we were never really able to create the singularity in Rays vision… but over the last few years, because of the volumes of raw, personal data we've been collecting via technology, we're edging closer. Could the movement I was part of in fact be, as Eric Schmidt once said, 'the largest experiment in anarchy that we have ever had'? In hindsight—I think so.

I think it's worth me saying in the introduction to this book, that trying to predict the future is largely a fool's game… and I say that as someone who seems to have ended up spending quite a lot of the last 20 years, of my professional life, being paid to do precisely this! If you'd asked me 20 years ago, to predict the things that exist today, I would never have got anywhere close to getting this right.

Not to mention new-ish emerging-ish tech', like Artificial Intelligence, Cryptocurrency and Blockchain, Virtual and Augmented Reality, The Internet of Things, Autonomous Vehicles, Drones and so on.

So we've established that I'm a completely rubbish futurist. But one thing I've always been good at, wherever I've been, was re-building: taking things apart and putting them back together in different ways. I've always bent toward creative problem-solving. Still to this day, when people label me stoic or grumpy, in reality, I'm just trapped in my own head, exploring what my gift is – my superpower to solve problems. I am—a *designer*.

Over the twenty years since I Forrest Gumped my way into that first job, I have zigzagged along a path of design where I've had to learn how to code, I've had to learn how to 'design *think*' and I've learned how to empathise with the consumers of many different products and industries. I've worked closely with psychologists, psychotherapists and neuroscientists. I've lobbied politicians and walked in the halls of some of the most significant companies in the world – selling and building this thing we call digital without ever genuinely understanding its potential. During this time there was always one thing that drove me, and it was this question… why?

This innate curiosity about why people were doing the things they were doing and *using* the stuff that we were building… was to me… interesting. Was there perhaps a psychological reason… why? Neurological reasons? Many of the things we created were entirely useless on the grand scale of things, but didn't stop people literally – eating – it – up. This word—why—kept emerging, as I watched and observed the way people were interacting with the things we were building and these *why* moments – without even realising it – were steering my design toward the philosophical. But was this even allowed in my field? During times of genuine concern, I would try talking to colleagues about all of this. I soon learned to keep my mouth shut.

Pete:	'Paula… why are we *doing* this?'
Paula:	'Doing what?'
Pete:	'*Designing* this?'
(Pause)	
Paula:	'Pete, stop being weird.'

Was I thinking in a way that school wouldn't have allowed? Because I was pushing the concept that we don't have knowledge of a thing until we have grasped its why. I was perpetually at a schism. On the one hand, I was a designer who was meant to let things loose, where quantity not quality was becoming more so the practice, but on the other hand – why? Why all of this? Why – why – why – why – why?

Why seemed to return during the silent moments on the commute back home, or in the shower, or chopping my carrots on a Sunday. Was my intuition secretly guiding me somewhere? I count myself lucky that each day I still get the opportunity to help make people's lives easier but when I've been in client's boardrooms, I've always felt slightly alone – unable to philosophise and talk about things that were not to say… the natural corollary. For example, why make people's lives easier? And define that word *easier*. Should, for example, convenience and ease replace human experience? I have had many 'whys' over these years and repressed them I have. The result of all that repression… this book.

My first twenty years in this thing called digital has been a golden age of personal computing. I was on the inside of a new industrial revolution and there was a compelling, straightforward logic behind a lot of the design thinking through this period. But the twenty years before I started working were full of more significant breakthrough moments for the digital age, and I've often wondered why the last twenty have been full of 'incremental' steps in interface design – as opposed to those monumental leaps. Apparently, civilisations move in this fashion, incrementally and then suddenly, everything quantum leaps.

During those two decades preceding my start, the world added monitors and keyboards to computers. We saw Moore's Law come true and the miniaturisation of semiconductors meant more power… in less space. Of course, the real coming-of-age moment was an idea born in the 1970s and realised to full force in the 80s and 90s, a shift which would humanise computers and turn them into everyone's current superpower: *The Graphical User Interface*. But as with all things, brilliant ideas need to evolve and move on and so it is my belief that because we've hung on so tightly and so strictly to the GUI, it's led to the creation of erroneous touch-points and a continuous optimisation and massaging of something that *was* great, as a means to an end… but in itself should never have been considered the end.

Each day in my industry, we're breaching new frontiers in science and technology, but for all the knowledge we have gathered, we've been surprisingly bad at handling the simple yet fundamental questions of what truly fulfils these human needs of ours. To know this, we must understand the human condition, and that was not part of my training in school—or anywhere. Instead, we tend to fall back on a simplistic, mechanical understanding of our desires and measure this and design to accommodate *this*.

For me, too many people have been designing the next version of something that exists, rather than trying to invent the best version of something new, something that is *relevant*. Without different perspectives, there is a real chance that the current approach to designing digital products may end up being built into the software that in fact runs our society and our lives – and if that happens, the ideology of a few design intellectuals will be amplified from novelty into a force that would colour our world with Isaac Asimov's paintbrush. Perhaps considering why Asimov's books should be read, as well as Kurzweil's, will help move the discussion away from quantity and convenience and onto a different path – a more human-focused one.

Lots of things have inspired me to think of design through a more human-focused lens. For example, the Krebs Cycle presents us with a map that describes the metabolic cycle. In this analogy, the four modalities of human creativity—Science, Engineering, Design and Art—replace the Krebs Cycle's carbon compounds. In an *Age of Entanglement*, Neri Oxmas states, that 'each of the modalities (or 'compounds') produces 'currency' by transforming into another'.

The Krebs cycle diagram is an excellent example of how people could start to expand our understanding of what good design is, by looking diagonally at more previously unrelated, environmental elements.

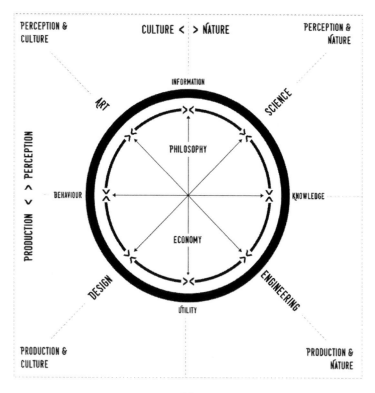

Apart from the slowly emerging philosophical conversation, there has been very little examination of the social effects digital tech has on us as a people and on civilisations as eco-systems. Sophie Deen an EduTech expert from the UK, recently shone a light on the fact that we may believe the world is more connected, but in reality, only forty percent of the world's people are connected to digital, and the divide is growing year on year. Human interaction with anything, be it digital or physical, requires us to look deeply at the challenge and ask the question, 'Is this universal or merely novel?' In other words, we need to align ourselves more closely with balance in the digital things we make with respect to the effects on us, and our relationship with them. To even begin to go there, we must first accept that we have not brought psychology into the discussion as much as we should have. In this sense, we have failed in a substantial way, and this is something we must admit first, then we can begin again, and explore territory we have tried so tactfully to bury.

As technology becomes increasingly immaterial, and we move from information delivery to the fulfilment of abstract tasks (rather than aiding human needs), I ask this: does the technology we've created just add more layers of confusion? When we strip away all the technology, what are we left with? I will argue it is the same thing we started with— people. But before we move into the deep weeds of my design philosophy, a few words of caution... I have a reductionist approach to life, design and philosophy. I'm just not intelligent enough to be complicated, but also, I'm going to argue forward my position on why this approach or way does have its strengths. Reductionism is how I've always approached design, with perhaps an odd balance of EQ / IQ. Ultimately, what I've always tried to avoid are overly complicated approaches to problem-solving, but in an industry that prides itself in complicated approaches to simple challenges, it's often forgotten and because of this, even some of the most widely used frameworks from the best design consultancies in the world baffle my mind. Occam's Razor reminds that 'when you have two competing theories that make the same predictions, the simpler one is the better', so even if the words in this book might at times feel a bit too deep and philosophical, it is in fact quite the opposite: for as we step back from the painting, breathe and re-look at what it all is, then we see what it is—just a vision of what could be.

I like looking at the little things because to solve a tiny challenge; I do it in a tiny way – based on a tiny insight. 'Nature operates in the shortest way possible,' wrote Aristotle, so is this not something to mirror? In the not too distant future, will digital design itself not be considered as quite a bizarre principle? Designing 'screens' to solve human challenges! Why not make the process more human by a leap and take away the screens? Use tech but without the parts? The buttons, the screens, the double-clicking. On that note, what *are* buttons, usernames and… *passwords*? If we know how to climb to the end without them and get to be where we want to be, why use them as the vehicle? Why not zip-line? What we will find is that a lot of factors in design are in fact fictions and things we've been too dogmatic about as leaders in this field. Because of this, I've alienated myself from a lot of the businesses and colleagues I've worked with, like a belligerent child; because I would often debunk a brief or supposed customer need based solely on my point-of-view that it didn't add anything – because it didn't take into account the routes of our human condition, and build to service them. And so there I was in the corner – asking that same question… why? Why design it? Why do anything? Unless it knows of the human drivers and services them – unless it does – will it not simply evaporate? Or demand patchwork and a whole journey of plastering? Yes, it will because that is what I have observed in two decades. It then re-enters the cycle, and like a soul entering a new body to learn lessons it didn't in its past life, it seems to travel through the system yet again. Instead of leaping forward, it exists on that lower fractal, spinning in a vortex. I've watched it happen again and again. And again, we build a better version of the thing.

us·er — yo oz∂r — noun

- A person who uses or operates something, esp. a computer or other machine.

- A person who takes illegal drugs; a drug user.

This is the thing: we're not users… we are people. We are not animals being farmed in an Orwellian dreamscape, we are conscious spirits – living, breathing entities – or have we forgotten? Maybe some of us didn't even know? It's mind – body – spirit, not mind – mind – mind.

Why do you all call your customers 'users'? I don't know. We've always called them that. Jack Dorsey, CEO, Square

We started using the word 'user' during the early days of modern computing. It was solidified by hackers, who used the term to refer to people who weren't technical or creative, but people who just consumed the digital things being made. In the 90s it was paired with other words to create whole new meanings. 'I invented the term because I thought Human Interface and usability were too narrow,' Don Norman said. 'I wanted to cover all aspects of the person's experience with a system, including industrial design, graphics, the interface, the physical interaction and the manual.'

It has not been uncommon throughout the senior manager years of my career to stop a designer mid-functional-description and ask them, 'how does the *person* using this thing feel?'

This… is what I want *you* to consider. Feelings, not functions.

For me, technology should fit around how people want to feel. Then it is for us to be servicing *that*, rather than us playing God and creating new behaviours or habits or being bent on doing things to then observe what happens, making notes and carrying on, as if we were wearing long white coats and our markets were there to be experimented on. In fact, we need do nothing of the sort, as all of this market research seems to have been done. But which tech design culture ever encourages the study of the epic poems, the bibles, historical record, philosophy and psychoanalysis? We return to the research process any polymath will take but is this method to progress in digital really necessary? Can coders benefit from the study of chi gong? Do designers need to read *The Republic*? Is there any benefit in teaching corporate bankers of The Hero's Journey? Is there an example of any mathematician turned poet? Yes, and in 1048, Omar Khayyam was born in North Eastern Iran. No more significant case could be put forward for the need to merge linear thought patterns with an organic approach than when observing the polymath who formulated algebra and wrote of mechanics, geography, mineralogy, music and Islamic theology. He described the beauty of nature in his poems, pure love and wine. The Persian genius was also an astronomer and philosopher, and elegist of a one thousand four-line-verse poem, proving in the medieval period that one didn't need to embrace language as one nor other, or that one didn't need to approach something, as linear or organic. His *Treatise on Demonstration of Problems of Algebra* is now considered one of the most critical disquisitions on algebra written before modern times.

That means this: not only is Dave, the coder in my company, allowed to pick up poems by Milton... he should.

As a passionate observer of cultural, economic and tech trends, I'm excited about the feeling that we're now at a critical turning point and if we can commit to a human-focused approach towards designing our future with technology, and by starting first to understand what it means to be human and approaching this organically, holistically, and amplifying our best qualities, and not just playing into our base chemical demands and building more apps that nobody needs—then a bright and powerful future is there for us to claim. We just need to align, return to balance – zero point – and all we reach for will manifest as fast as the noise comes when we click our fingers. Amongst the hysteria of the digital revolution, we forgot we are human. Not anymore.

The most exciting breakthroughs of the 21st century will not only occur because of technology but because of an expanding concept of what it means to be human. John Naisbitt

Moving away from terms like 'user' and being more human is going to be difficult because it's so ingrained in our industry now. In general psychology, there is a principle called the *availability bias*, which means we perceive something to be more important the more we are subjected to it and made aware of it. The tendency to overvalue what is—and undervalue what could be—forms the basis of much of our industries ethics. A lot of the time, the judgments we make, and why we make them, come not from critical thought or personal experience, but from the mere existence of that something in the first place. Like the term 'user'. As a result, things that already get a lot of attention tend to stay popular and often seem to serve as the perfect point of entry. But it's time to question those biases and realign.

It is as all of the philosophers have taught, where all psychology has returned to, and all art forms have been the creations for. It is the pursuit of one thing that underpins all the fundamental questions we have ever asked, and it can be summarised in just two words: 'know thyself'.

1. WE'RE NOT DIGITISING BEHAVIOUR; WE'RE BEHAVING IN A DIGITAL WORLD!

'If you need something from somebody always give that person a way to hand it to you.' Sue Monk Kidd

It will be up to people, not machines or technology, to create a future for design and technology – one that is so desirable in its function that we will look back at the last twenty years nostalgically and reflect in a bittersweet fashion—seeing only our naivety. Much in the same way that our spoiled eyes would watch VHS now and wonder how we ever coped before *DVD*, we watch HD with ease – it is the norm but as far as VHS is concerned, how did we ever bear it? For Don Norman, anything that is created by human beings is a technological artefact, whether physical (tangible objects, e.g. paper) or mental (information structures, e.g. language), dividing technological innovations into good and evil, or those that 'make us smart' and those that literally 'make us stupid' by frustrating and enslaving us. Emerging technologies are not the danger, but the failure of human imagination, optimism, energy, and creativity is. The central claim of a lot of people is that technology makes us forget what we already know about life. It precludes our developing fully independent selves. We cannot cope with human relationships unmediated by algorithms and filters, and we stare at our phones and the real world streams past unnoticed and unappreciated—true to a certain extent, but why can't we build a world where technology does things that are wonderful things? One that will focus more of our attention? It's easy to point the finger and say 'not good', but it's hard to rebuild, and this is what we are entering, a phase of technological revisionism while at the same time catching the fresh wave that has risen from the surface and is screaming to be surfed.

People often ask me what the future of design and technology looks like. First I tell them the truth: I don't know. But what I do know is that it's going to be a lot better than it has been until now and I want to help create a world full of Don's 'make us smart' technologies and you're going to have to want to go there too. With the vast increase in different devices over the past few years, it's safe to assume that the future will provide a host of new screens and interfaces for us to play with. As the Internet of Things gathers pace, there will be many more screens to look at, and it will be our job to make sure they're as human-friendly as possible. Designing a future that acknowledges that we all change and evolve is a good first step because, with that, future proofing is a safer place to enter.

This concept of future proofing is illustrated by Steward Brand regarding building design: a young couple might buy a house, decorate a room as a nursery, create a study area for teenagers, install an office and a flat for their parents and a well-designed building will allow for all these changes as it in itself now thinks how space can be re-organised. Brand outlines this approach to architecture in his book, *How Buildings Learn*, which speaks of good architecture acknowledging that spaces will be used in different ways over time: the space plan always being in a constant state of flux. In much the same way, we want to design for all the possible changes we can foresee and make our services flexible enough to accommodate changes we can't envisage at the time but do have the possibility to play out into the future. We can build design systems that will self-think and are thus always able to offer ideas about how things can be used and re-structured to best accommodate anything we want.

Being future-proof means acknowledging that when the screen world changes so rapidly, we need to focus more on the information that comes out of the interfaces, rather than obsessing over the detail of each screen. The interfaces need to go away to make the future of interaction design even viable. But what is an interface? 'In its simplest sense, the word interface refers to software that shapes the interaction between user and computer,' according to Steven Johnson in *Interface Culture: How New Technology Transforms the Way We Create and Communicate*. 'The interface serves as a kind of translator, mediating between the two parties, making one sensible to the other.'

Think of the physical computer screen as representing the embodiment of the invisible cyberspace – and as such it is a way for people to make sense of and use the hidden world that's otherwise beyond their grasp – the digital unconscious! Interface designers are hence the interpreters and tour guides to this realm, facilitating access to it through their endeavours.

We've had a lot of practice at interaction design and brought a lot of nontechnical people along on the digital journey through it. The human story is one of using technology to extend our senses, and our selves and various existing interface designs have been more or less successful in this way, by providing a way to share our experiences with others across the world. But approaches to interface design continue to evolve, and the challenge now becomes whether to address short-term audience requirements or attempt to predict how our needs will change in the longer term. In a swiftly changing technological world, can we spot the key trends and designs for just those developments without being distracted or heading up the wrong avenue? The answer will necessarily differ, depending on the nature of the problem being addressed. But the most successful designs in the future will have taken these human factors into account – it's just a case of selecting the right ones. Those that aim to make life easier for busy people, such as near field technology, are already addressing how we want to live our lives and are providing solutions in a seamless, invisible, human way.

My hope for the future of technology is that it disappears, it gets out of the way, and it somehow amplifies the best qualities of humanity. Instead of us all zooming further into the interface experience and locking ourselves into that and saying 'this is technology, this is what it is', we now have the chance to climb out of our Plato caves and be in the world, while allowing technology to serve us while we are, instead of us just connecting our bodies to it. People don't need digital experiences that complete them: they need digital experiences that understand them completely. Welcome to a future where humans are back in the driver's seat, and where gadgets have lost their power over us and technology is more seamlessly woven into the fabric of our lives.

Our machines should be nothing more than a tool for extending the powers of the humans who use them. Thomas Watson, Jr.

Up until now, the goal of design in our field has centred on the screen, its development and the changing ways in which we use it. Our computers, ATM machines, mobile phones and even household alarm systems all have the characteristic feature of a screen. Touchscreen technology seemed to herald the way for Minority Report-style interfaces and yet... increasingly we're exploring other ways to interact with the Internet of Things – using voice activation and gesture recognition that threaten the primacy of the screen in our lives. Further, the technology we now dream of creating will free us from the need to interact with it at all as it begins to anticipate our needs – ordering in our organic veg, as our fridge notifies us we're running low. Meanwhile, we'll be spending time with friends and family, on our hobbies and we will have time again to build, write, study and know of the self once more, as we'll experience the kind of self-actuation that is possible when the mundane everyday chores are taken care of. To build a genuinely human-focused future, we must stop designing for people as if they were machines.

But isn't being human-focused precisely what we've seen take centre stage these last few years? Admittedly, the rise of the 'User Experience' community championing more objective design processes and the undeniable power of things like the sharing economy have been signs of an economic system increasingly geared towards human needs and desires? The removal of conventional barriers to communication as a result of much of the population having access to the Internet has undoubtedly brought benefits regarding collaboration and new opportunities to explore the world, either virtually or in real life. Designers and providers of services need to be aware that one consequence is that their customers have high – some might say impossibly high – expectations in terms of requiring an instant response provided without cost to them, which they will publicly grade to mark their satisfaction. We ignore their part in the dynamic at our peril.

If you are a start-up looking to create something that is not just a passing fad, but indeed reaches deep into the future, ask yourself if the idea you hold is serving the audience's ability to self-optimise *into* a human as an augmented machine, or does it provide an opportunity to self-actualise as a human who relates to the world around him through his search for meaning? Does it encourage a person to know thyself, or return to Plato's cave and suppress consciousness in a dark and restricted experience? Plato's Allegory of the Cave – are our phones and tablets, modern day examples of it?

In a near version of the future, based on the fact that we—as humanity—are living lifestyles that are unsustainable for our health and our consumption, a better set of methods will emerge. There's a discrepancy between the level we consume, the resources we have, and the lifestyles we are living and nature have a return to balance mechanism that will re-position us. We have begun to see the mental health conditions rise and old ones re-emerge, so if we don't want utter chaos, if we want to take action and find a direction that leads to a sustainable lifestyle for all beings, our approach to design must change— from our attitudes toward consumption to our understanding of the word happiness.

Scanning the world vista of all cultures today – and not just among the young – it doesn't seem to be the case that such a balance is being met – as pleasure calls for more pleasure, and in the modern day advertising landscape where sex sells, consumption is happiness and more is better (especially that little bit more than everyone else) are we able to find that balanced sweet spot? Or have we lost it forever? Also, happiness is neither a permanent state of being nor is it a zone that can be arrived at. It is therefore not surprising that advertising sells its products to increase our 'happiness', as a customer will need to keep coming back for more, and then a little bit more. We didn't evolve to be satisfied, we evolved to survive and reproduce, and evolution is indifferent to whether we are suffering or not. Perhaps, even though we like to be happy, we need to change the focus to working out who we are, and how we can alleviate stress, lift the pressure of experiencing temporary thrills that masquerade as balance.

Technology can help us here. Especially if we don't *fear* it.

2. DESIGN AND HUMANS

'Adapt yourself to the things among which your lot has been cast and love sincerely the fellow creatures with whom destiny has ordained that you shall live.' Marcus Aurelius

design — dɪˈzʌɪn — noun

- a plan or drawing produced to show the look and function of a building, garment, or other object before it is made — "good design can help the reader understand complicated information" — the arrangement of the features of an artefact, as produced from following a plan or drawing.

- purpose or planning that exists behind an action, fact, or object — "the appearance of design in the universe."

- synonyms: intention, aim, purpose, plan, intent, objective, object, goal, end, target, point, hope, desire, wish

In the English language, the word 'design' takes on a variety of noun and verb meanings. In its noun, standard dictionaries indicate concepts of sketch, drawing, plan, pattern, intention or purpose, or the art of producing them. In its verb, the same dictionaries indicate elements of definition – involving representing an artefact, system or society, or the fixing of its look, function or purpose. The word design, therefore, has meanings ranging from the abstract conception of something to the actual plans and processes required to achieve it.

I believe there are only two design paradigms: i) technology-driven design and ii) human-focused design. That is to say, something designed to fix a human condition, support humans, protect humans, show them affection, understand them, allow them to participate, help them find leisure, encourage them to create, give them a sense of identity and give them a sense of—freedom. But over the years since I've been part of the industry, we've taken the technology-driven approach as the primary route more often than not. Even without realising it, most designers are *functionally* fixated and push frantically to make better versions of things they have seen before. We help tech find a problem, rather than problems find a solution because *analytical linear thought is confined to the tunnel it lives within.* A more holistic approach to design is inevitably becoming the only option. Being process driven is an important half, but being open to more is the everything.

human — hjuːmən — adjective

- relating to or characteristic of humankind — "the human body"

- of or characteristic of people, as opposed to God or animals or machines, especially in being susceptible to weaknesses — "they are only human, and therefore mistakes do occur."

- synonyms: compassionate, humane, kind, kindly, kind-hearted, considerate, understanding, sympathetic, tolerant

Much has been written over the years about the topics of User Centred Design and Human Centred Design. Wikipedia states that:

'Human-centred design has its roots in fields such as ergonomics, computer science and Artificial Intelligence. The echoes of this past can be noted in international standards such as ISO 9241-210 "Ergonomics of human-centred system interaction", which describes human centred design as "an approach to systems design and development that aims to make interactive systems more usable by focusing on the use of the system

and applying human factors/ergonomics and usability knowledge and techniques".'

The *robotically* titled *ISO 9241-210* specifically recommends five characteristics for a human-centred system:

1. The adoption of multidisciplinary skills and perspectives
2. Explicit understanding of *users*, tasks and environments
3. *User*-centred evaluation driven/refined design
4. Consideration of the whole *user* experience
5. Involvement of *users* throughout design and development.

Even the most famous design company in the world – IDEO – uses the term Human Centred Design to describe its process and approach to problem-solving. In their description, they define it as being 'as much about your head as your hands'. It is the design philosophy behind their approach to creative problem solving and shows people that how they think about design directly affects whether they'll arrive at innovative, impactful solutions or not. IDEO work with the people they're designing for by building a deep knowledge of their customers, developing prototypes along the way and closing with new solutions tailored to their needs. It's lovely in theory, but more human-focused digital should focus on what makes us humans, not focus on what makes us users. As Simon Norris, managing director at Nomensa, a design consultancy that combines psychological insight with design, says: *'Great design requires great psychology. Psychology is the science of behaviour and the mind. When design and behaviour match, the design will be superior.'* So ask yourself the big question—what makes us behave? If we truly understand what makes us human, what triggers us, and why, then we would be designing differently and in respect to that, rather than the 'user' interfaces of today.

Historical record contains numerous examples of successful devices that required people to adapt to and learn from such devices. People were expected to acquire a good understanding of the activities to be performed, and of the operation of the technology and because of this, we can then affirm that people adapt to the tools they are using, and not the other way around. Paul Davies, CEO of the psychology-led design consultancy Behaviour, states, *'Unlike artists, designers have to make something that fixes a problem; an artist can start a project without a brief, but a designer has to have a purpose, and they have to do that for a particular audience. There's a common adage that designers are artists who can't draw, I would argue that designers are psychologists who can draw.'*

Our most significant flaw up until now with human-focused design solutions has been our inability to adapt to each person carefully, and it was science fiction to think we could do that *intelligently* – but the technology just caught up. Whilst the individual is a moving target and designing for that individual of today means the design will probably be wrong tomorrow (everything is in a constant state of emergence, change, flux), I believe we do now have the right pieces in place to start (at the very least) thinking about a design world that does adapt and change to each person. If this is in itself a problem to solve, I have realised from my re-building days that a lot of time can, in fact, be wasted beginning to re-build a thing when the thing in and of itself is not necessary to start with.

Realising what is relevant first and then grounding ourselves in that seat is the right first mark to hit, else this bull in the china shop approach to design will now begin to contribute nothing as the design world has— for many of us—arrived at a place, where unless we pause and inflect, shiny lights on sneakers will macro out and human progress will be forgotten as our handle on what we are and what we want and need— with respect to progress—will become a lost target within the bamboozling, and bombarding world of sneakers with shiny lights on.

I am a person. I want to get from A-C via B. B is a piece of technology that enables a transition. To make B effective, you need to understand the psychological factors of A (the driver) to make sure B (the vehicle) gets you to C (your destination).

In understanding the psychological factors of A, we will know if we even want to ride B to C. Sometimes, when addressing the route of the A, we lift immense amounts of pressure, tasks and graft from our schedules because, nobody ever wanted to do 'A' to begin with! We just thought we did. In addressing A, we understood A. Do you want to get on that train or have you just been sold the idea of 'The Island'? In the science fiction film set in 2019, Lincoln Six Echo and Jordan Two Delta live in a compound. Residents believe that the outer world has become too contaminated for human life… with the exception of *The Island*. Each week a lottery is played, and the winner leaves the compound to live on the paradise island, which they are shown video feeds of a heaven on earth. Due to the possibility of winning, inhabitants are kept 'hoping'. They have after all committed to the idea of The Island for many years, so aren't going to quit suddenly. Through entrainment, the collective of inhabitants support the myth of The Island, and the hope self-perpetuates out of necessity. The hope of a better day, belief in progress, and faith in a fictitious utopia, instead of grounding the self into the now and being here – in this reality.

Human-focused digital is that apex between technology and interface. How can we make the technology more human centred and the way it is consumed feel more human? Surely we must look at the things that make us human? For a long time, we've been too hung up on the interface, and unable to articulate the technology, obsessing over the ergonomics and the usability of the artefacts and information we produce. As the information sciences started to become more critical to the experiences we created, the design world evolved and that's why more human-focused systems are going to now be key: so for technology, interface and information science to converge at a deeper level, we must take the cross-disciplinary approach to design and revise why we did 'A', want to do 'A' and what 'A' is.

Our industry is made up of many disciples from computer science, sociology, psychology, the cognitive sciences, anthropology, communication studies, and graphic design all the way to industrial design. Considering the relevance of the fundamental questions that underpin our discussion, shouldn't that group expand out to include philosophers, artists, writers and storytellers? This is the first thing: to incorporate those holistic creative minds who 'feel' more and then to merge a balanced entrance in with a practice of designing for the lowest common denominator—and not showing off with our logical, analytical egos. It is time to bring in the rare Myers-Briggs INFP's, and not forget the necessity of the rare group who introvert, intuit, feel and perceive because Shakespeare, Tolkien, Orwell, Aldous Huxley, Kierkegaard, C.S. Lewis, Virginia Woolf, J.K. Rowling, Kafka, Edgar Allan Poe, Milton, Blake and Van Gough were all of this rare calibration, and somehow able to access very profoundly an ocean of design and shape to present back to humanity the thing we are all struggling to understand—everything. Incorporating creative artists is for many a low entry point, especially when big design corporations can employ top computer scientists and rocket engineers because they are the ones who are intelligent—but remember, there are many different types of intelligence.

We must be interested in design that is capable of understanding the person or people who know the least, not the *most* – so testing out work with two types of people – children and pensioners might be an excellent place to start. They're the least technical people you know and at the same time, the wisest, having learnt nothing or unlearnt everything, and therefore using them as the consumer of all digital design work is the easiest way of defining something enjoyable for all others. As well as stepping back and learning from people, designers must not hesitate to shed this linear, analytical ego and go one stage further. Letting go, next becomes the most effective method to sustainable progress because people, you will find, figure out how to solve issues on their own.

Trust then can become the default position of your design practice, and trusting that the collective feedback of markets will not only co-ordinate your design forward more efficiently but in letting go and not leading, the feedback data, in fact, becomes an ocean of knowledge and within that – there is data and within that – patterns emerge, ones you were previously not considering. It can then be more natural to edge and lead forward once these patterns are in position and, as long as the human condition is continuously catered for and encouraged, you may find yourself edging people ahead not only in a way that it becomes highly efficient as a work method, but it is for the benefit of the whole. Thus, the trajectory has revealed itself and you as a designer can stand back, fold arms and observe the beauty of a growth pattern you have structurally engineered and do less, not more, to get there.

Human-focused design is about helping to identify the things you need to do for people to help them get to the root of the problem, and then stepping aside. Instead of playing 'doctor', practise the letting go principle and enjoy watching that the body will in fact self-heal and self-align. To summarise, people will find their own solutions and conventions within your general framework. People, you see, can be compared to the humble sardine, especially in modern society. When we take one sardine out of the tin, that seems to allow space for another to move, breathe and live – to swim off in the direction it knew to anyway – the direction that its inner compass was wanting to take it off in all along. When left, life will naturally align with what is harmonious to flow. If you prevent breathing and space to 'be', you are hurting, cornering and snookering and you are creating a huge amount of work for yourself as you then try so hard to motivate and encourage. You then try to draw blood out of a stone and give in, sit back and exhale in exhaustion. What just happened? It's about this: don't do things better, do better things. In other words, try less, don't force – and be. Observe also yourself and question why you are doing what you are, what your motivations are to force a design through and don't judge yourself, just observe and answers will emerge, you yourself will re-align and consequently, so will your design work and any results of your genius harmonious blueprints.

Science fiction has always predicted that technology would dominate and triumph over the imperfect nature of the human being and that we would reach new heights of health and perfectionism but is this review and observation of our imperfect nature something we should build to accommodate or something we should just accept? That the human condition is not perfect? And that there is nothing wrong with that, and that reaching into utopian futures has in fact been forever the forerunner for forceful and ego-driven regimes. Is the emergence of new technologies perhaps in-fact something to flow within its emergence in a balance, while we evolve? Is it not for us both to evolve in parallel? New technologies have an ability to steer us towards greater self-realisation, and that must surely be the case – otherwise, why would digital tech exist? If it didn't evolve out of ingenuity as a natural evolutionary emergence, why is it with us? That being said, if it is not here to aid in our evolutionary journey to 'know thyself', to clear us of pollutions, to sustain our earth planet and to harness clean energies, then why is it here? If it is not here to help and aid, then it will dissolve away.

With this in mind, we are all collectively in the perfect win-win scenario and because of this – mothers can relax about how much their kids are playing with their iPads – and they can assure themselves now that it will basically sort itself out. Nature has a way of finding this balance. If digital tech can't help us progress, it will run its course and similarly, if it is to continue, it will do so bending toward nurturing *our* progress, so fear not the rise of the machines. Meanwhile, in a funny way, that fear and paranoia can in fact conjure those very machines! In her book *No Go The Bogeymen*, Marina Warner examines the presence of male terror figures in song and story, establishing their origins in mythology. Used as frightening monsters to lessen or represent 'the very terrors that our sleep of reason conjures up,' Warner shows how the bogeymen unfold with strategic purpose, warning us of the dangers our ignorance plays when we reproduce the monster, like the Bogeymen in Terry Pratchett's comic fantasy series *Discworld* where the monster appears as an anthropomorphic personification of children's fears. Without fear, no monster would manifest, but as the psychologists knew it, with fear, anything can be created. The paranoia and hysteria of x, creates—x.

What about this instead – if we're on this digital tech curve of growth, then why not grow according to the service of improved health and well being? And not our narcissisms, hedonisms and dopamine reward systems? Remember, it's no longer about 'we're designing this because it's fun', but about looking at 'A'. Books, papers and frameworks on this introversion are emerging, and the pairing of design and these conditions in our discussions could encourage the sea change during this crucial junction in digital and design, technology and product. It's happening anyway, the wave has come now, and surfers the world over are telling their neighbour surfer buddies to wax up, because it's going to be a big one. It's not only coming—it's here.

We're seeing a fascinating nexus of ideas and methods all starting to converge to a point of intelligence that we've never witnessed. Technology just learnt how to interpret human behaviours, so things like Behavioural Economics have moved mainstream and onto the path of user experience and digital design. We're in a time now and the opportunity is here for us to do one of two things: good… or bad…

From as far back as memory reaches, people have been telling other people what's good for them, and manipulating or forcing them to do this, that and the other based on imbalanced, out of flow ambitions – but this is not sustainable. The human spirit and natural flow always outs, so why design against it? Tricking people to do *anything* that they wouldn't normally do, even under the guise of 'being helpful' is age-old in literature and mythology – the archetypal Pied Piper shows that leading a person down the garden path with extravagant promises will always lose out to the innate spirit of intuition, and the direction the inner compass is guiding us all in. Genuinely servicing others with nothing but integrity and harnessing the moral compass will always win during any sea change, so surfing the right wave over that gorgeous ocean is what will lead you successfully to the horizon. Only then will others follow. Doing good or bad, it's easy, obvious and innate. I know though, it's difficult in today's world, isn't it? Yes, we *are* lost… and confused among the tidal wave of mixed messages on how to best be…

I can still recall the tiny smirk on my face when I watched the movie 'Her' for the first time. I fell in love with how seamlessly the technology in that film was able to fill the cracks in Theodore Twombly's life. We could have that if we really wanted it. We just have to design in a different way. With most digital design, we wouldn't normally worry about the *environment* that it enters. We just release something into the wild, observe its impact and evolve it. However, with the subtle changes that Ai based design start to introduce and the fact we need to design more personality than interface, it starts to change the game a lot. We're about to enter what I'm calling the age of '*Anthropomorphic Digital*'. Anthropomorphism refers to things designed with the attribution of human traits and emotions. These are the products that will inevitably elicit responses from others. Anthropomorphic design can have obvious advantages, for instance, the human-shaped scarecrow which frightens off the birds. But when we start to introduce anthropomorphic digital products into our lives and homes it can be like introducing a new person into the household, which doesn't always go as smoothly as a family might hope.

AUTONOMOUS CONTROL

SERVICE (DO IT FOR ME WHEN I COMMAND)	**PERCEPUTAL** (KNOW WHAT I WANT, BEFORE I KNOW IT + TAKE CARE OF IT FOR ME)
SUPPORTIVE (HELP ME DO IT / FIND IT WHEN I ASK)	**PREDICTIVE** (ANTICIPATE MY NEEDS & SUGGEST OPTIONS)

RATIONAL (left axis) — **EMOTIONAL** (right axis)

MANUAL CONTROL

It's going to be a very delicate balance to find and the designers capable of looking outside of the circle will quickly become the most sought after as they base products on the innate human psyche and not the repetitive, learned behaviour approach to tasks that we've tricked ourselves into believing is the method of success. Learning to fit this new emerging type of Anthropomorphic Digital into the daily lives of real people without it become another great attack on the senses is a really fascinating challenge.

Cities: great metropolises? Or communication pollution farms? Is it the bombardment of messages and promises of sex, money, power and fame that are attracting us as designers to perpetuate the growth of anxiety and speed? The bombardment of mixed messages may appear heavy – because this is its intention. If it is heavy, and present and there – and all of the time – we may think that it is real, true, and eventually its message relevant, knowing, correct. The advertising technique is simple – this is the truth and if you don't believe it now, wait and I shall repeat – four thousand times a second. Think of it as a million voices screaming and the person who can scream the loudest wins, the loudest voice is the one you can hear, because it drowns out all the other voices. Subsequently, you don't know what the others are saying, only what the loud voice is saying: it is the only information that exists, so it must be selected. Cities: a twenty-four-hour joy ride odyssey. By the end of the workday – we go to splat in front of a box that provides only the rations that an exhausted and stressed human brain can wrestle. Too exhausted to think, we switch from channel to channel, zoning out of one programme and into the next television *programme*. Coping with this situation and navigating our way through the bombardment maze is necessary to finding the relaxed state. Being more relaxed, less stressed, less tense and generally less the model to an Edward Munch canvas will make us better at designing in a way that encourages a person's well-being. When we are tense and worried and trembling, and products of our city metropolises, our designs will project those states out.

Being less susceptible to biases and building out of a place that is grounded in nurturing human progress may sound easy… but when the biology of our human brain is too easily affected by environmental stimulants… to wheat, to coffee, to sugar, to advertisements of Jennifer Lopez, the real challenge begins. The question is this: how do we find peace and build in positive changes that are based on the human needs and designed with familiar human traits? Sometimes, merely looking at what not to do, can open a space for where we should step. First closing the doors on the *no's* will introduce the doors that are *yes*. Then it becomes about this: braving up, climbing forward—and moving on.

3. THE HUMAN APPROACH
(AND THE ONLINE DATING OF NO)

'If music be the food of love, play on.' Shakespeare, Twelfth Night

The questions are: i) are we in control of our digital lives? And ii) by understanding the self, can we give people more sovereignty through digital design?

As stated, we've spent too long focusing digital design too broadly on the ergonomics and the usability of computing artefacts and the collection, manipulation, and use of information. What we need is a conversation that starts to bridge the gaps between the disciplines involved with the design and implementation of technology that supports human activity, because *design should be about a set of behaviour driven methodologies that apply to any function that uses technology which people interact with directly to accomplish a goal using personal devices.* This can include the use of tablets, phones and the more ambient devices that use natural language to engage people in conversation.

For me, one thing has always maintained, from watching the brilliant people at the helicopter factory to the fantastic people I'm surrounded by today at the very top tables of industry and that is the underlying feeling that we have been doing all of this—wrong, playing into the culture of consumerism and not for any productive mentality.

There is little doubt that the changes wrought by digital on our lives have been anything other than profound and in a recent survey by the World Economic Forum, roughly two-thirds of respondents said that digital media use had improved their ability to learn and develop professionally. However, the way we consume media in this digital method needs to be considered—and managed well. But even approaching operating or maintaining this, we need to understand the *extent* of the consumption, the types of interactions (both interface and social) and the types of content. Of course, we already employ colossal data analytic teams and tag our designed products to gather vast lakes of information, but this is usually driven by the urge to optimise and therefore sell more. Selling more is not vital though if selling things is producing negative impacts on experiences offline—in the *real*. Roughly four out of ten people report positive effects on attention span, long-term memory, stress and health and the ability to connect with people offline. But one in ten people reports those same areas are being negatively affected. Results also varied by country: in Germany, just thirty percent agreed that digital media usage improved the quality of life. Indeed, some of the great thinkers of our times are also starting to turn their backs on aspects of this digital estate we've built. Jared Newman at Fast Company recently announced his decision to ditch streaming music because 'there's a significance that comes with spending money on a particular song or album. It becomes an investment, which in turn demands your attention. I used to savour new tunes, listening to them over and over to identify their nuances.' Services like Spotify make the music feel disposable, he states.

Let's recap. We flooded the market with designed, technological experiences. We piped messages onto the computers we put in people's pockets; we connected people from different parts of the globe in ways that made the planet smaller. Rewind a few years before Skype – we were just about managing to coordinate the cheapest and most convenient way to call someone overseas via text message (which was also expensive). 'Let's keep it to fifteen minutes so the bill doesn't cripple me,' we'd say. The world was brilliant then, it is brilliant now, and it will be brilliant tomorrow. It is all, always perfect, in a state of total perfection while at the same time in a constant emergent state of the same. It is our awareness of that, which fluctuates. I love what we've created, but the point is: when you give Prometheus matches, expect some fires and it's not that the fires are wrong or that fire = bad, it is more the natural propensity or result of A. In defence of technology and human progress, Louis C.K. chastises society for failing to appreciate all the progress that has been made and the incredible lives technology has enabled us to lead. 'Those were simpler times I think. I just feel like, we may be going back to that by the way… in a way good because when I read things like the foundations of capitalism are shattering, I'm like maybe we need that. Maybe we need some time where we're walking around with a donkey with pots clanging on the sides… everything is amazing right now, and nobody's happy.' Louis C.K. is also an INFP personality (introversion, intuition, feeling, perception). It's time, it would seem, to introvert ourselves, if only a little. Perpetual extroversion only leads to the production and consumption of more and it's not for us to take production, nor progress, for granted as the effects some of this is *eventually* having on us are detrimental, with the potential to neurologically degenerate and environmentally ruin. This all needs to be realised.

Less than a decade after the introduction of the first iPhone, more people reach for their smartphones first thing in the morning than for a coffee, a toothbrush or even their partner lying next to them. Bombarded by notifications of new messages, social media posts, breaking news, app updates and *more*, we are disconnecting ourselves from some of the other essential things. Like everything, life is about balance. Parents are distracted by work emails at the dinner table, and gatherings of old friends can't do a couple of hours in a Pizza Express without checking their Gmail every ten minutes. Has it not the potential to suck the life out of us all? The convenience of not having to learn such things as how to read maps correctly may not have been the balanced pay-off we thought we were buying into.

Researchers at the University of British Columbia conducted an experiment with 221 people, asking them to participate in a two-week study. These were regular people with no apparent or diagnosed mental health conditions. During the first week, they asked half the participants to minimise phone interruptions by activating the 'do-not-disturb' setting and keeping their phones out of sight and far from reach. What they measured next was fascinating. Participants were interviewed to find out if they had experienced any of the eighteen symptoms of

ADHD (symptoms as specified by the *American Psychiatric Association*). The inattentiveness questions highlighted a range of problems: forgetting to pay bills, and having difficulty concentrating or listening. The hyperactivity questions assessed habits of fidgeting, sensations of restlessness, and a propensity toward excessive talking, even at the expense of interrupting other people to do so.

The results merely underline our suspicions. More frequent phone interruptions make people less attentive and more hyperactive. The data that these kinds of tests provide us with conclude that the continuous stream of digital stimulation we push at people is contributing to an increasingly problematic deficit of attention in people. It all backs up the prerequisite for rewrites in our designs.

It would be accurate to say we are *hopelessly* distracted by our phones, and *helplessly* devoted to them. Like conquered territory, our hands and minds are occupied: texting, tweeting, liking, emailing, sharing, Candy Crushing, and clicking on YouTube. Our state is one of split attention and divided sympathies; we find ourselves constantly and unstoppably stimulated. For a lot of us, the phone is the last thing we look at before sleep and the first thing we look at when we wake, and when it's not around us, we feel like we're missing a limb. What will happen next?

In the sci-fi movie *Children of Men*, Theo Farron (Clive Owen) has a cousin, a wealthy businessman, whose son is connected to his technological mobile device biologically and operates only in a zombified state of *consciousness* – plugged into Robert Nozick's 'The Experience Machine' (his phone) through the wrist, like the intravenous feed. His father calls to him twice before SCREAMING at his boy – to wake him from his trance-like state while he is 'connected' to his preferred 'real' world. Farron stares over the boy vacantly—'What has happened to us as a species?' his face begs. I can't help but share the confusion of this character when travelling on the tube, the buses, when drinking beers with friends, attending lectures or visiting museums. Sometimes I catch myself lost in a trance. Sometimes I catch people watching me. 'You see them staggering down our streets, heads bowed as if in prayer making the occasional grunting noise,' political satirist Will Durst writes in *Our Phone Obsession Is Turning Us Into Zombies*. 'Mindless drooling de-animated human husks walking blindly into fountains, crosswalks and lamp posts. Wake up people, we are in the middle of a science fiction movie here.'

Denying this self-evident trance that has grown among us is, in fact, a product of the trance, and the denial, although comfortable—is detrimental to our health, psychologically and physically. Deep down, we all know this. The irony is that the route of this denial is as natural as the blue sky deepening at night. To realise what is happening – the damage of The Experience Machine – are we required to unplug entirely? If so, why is it proving impossible? In an introduction to logic and the scientific method, Cohen and Nagel state, 'our emotional dispositions make it very difficult for us to accept certain propositions, no matter how strong the evidence in their favour. And since all proof depends upon the acceptance of certain propositions as true, no proposition can be proved to be true to one who is sufficiently determined not to believe it.' Cognitive dissonance is a psychological phenomenon that prevents people from accepting a reality irrespective of the amount of supporting evidence there is to support it.

⌘

Where there are too many choices, according to Barry Schwartz's *Paradox of Choice*, the risk is that we make no decision at all, or having made the decision, we now live out that chosen experience in a miserable state of not being completely satisfied. The perfect choice is never, it seems, complete enough. In *Is Too Much Choice Ruining Dating? Science Might Have the Answer* published on Mic, Ellie Krupnick asked a broad swathe of online daters about their experience—their answers were shockingly similar:

Daniel, 27, *"I often think that given fewer options, I'd be more likely to raise the ante and give something a real opportunity that I otherwise would not."*

Leah, 26, *"Every date you go on, you are already aware that you have other options waiting in your queue. The pressure is off, which is nice, but so is the incentive to try. When I first started dating, I would dress up nicely, do my hair, freshen my makeup. Now I barely attend to what I wear on dates, and if the date goes poorly, I can just check my dating apps on the train home."*

There's something else going on in those experiences too, something even more remarkable, something even more human:

You're on a dating app, and you've just found three people in proximity to you that you find 'attractive', so you've swiped them – to let them know you're nearby and interested – and the chain-reaction of events in your biology begins. Remembering that this story of the modern dating ritual didn't exist until a few years back, we're about to observe an entirely new, uncharted set of triggers, behaviours and reactions designed in an app-developers head and released into the wild (with little thought beyond the potential to change the dating game). You close the app, start to slide your phone back into your pocket and then something happens... the phone vibrates. Somebody likes you. Or do they? In an ocean of adrenaline, you wait: it has finally come... a response, and anxiety and joy combine. Between you reaching for the phone and unlocking, the brain region that is responsible for coordinating hormones, the hypothalamus, tells the adrenals to produce more testosterone and in turn confidence and therefore hunger for risk has surged. We can think of attraction as a feeling, or consider its possibility as being some form of pseudo high, a self-fulfilling prophecy of primal, digital joy that turns all the winners into—adrenaline junkies.

Under stress, cortisol manages functions of movement, respiration, sensitivity, growth, reproduction, excretion and our ability to digest and synthesise raw minerals and vitamins, amino acids and fats. This affects health and ultimately—the immune system. It's why stress can lead to heart attacks. Cortisol can injure the heart, liver, spleen, production of melatonin or the way the thyroid gland regulates mental well-being. In the brain, cortisol, like testosterone, has the initial beneficial effects of increasing arousal and sharpening attention, even promoting a slight thrill from the challenge, but as levels of the hormone rise and remain elevated, it comes to have the opposite effect. There is a difference between short-term and long-term exposure to a hormone, and that is a critical distinction to remember. Overexposure to any hormone will, in turn, produce abnormal bodily symptoms and for this reason, a bodybuilder when manipulating or influencing their hormonal levels will develop physical attributes in the bones, muscles and organs that are out of 'balance'. It's ironic, because that is precisely what they are striving for, symmetry and balance.

A lot of the digital services we're designing, either by choice or by accident (likely accident), are promoting the production of cortisol by prolonging actions and events across extended periods. I've spent a lot of time working in financial services, and one of the areas I studied was the effect of stress on the brain. 'Hippocampal Atrophy' is something normally associated with memory-loss conditions, such as dementia and Alzheimer's disease, and exposure to long-term stress causes it. Meditative practices do seem to have their benefit, but in a world moving as fast as ours, it's not that easy to sustain. Environmental pressures, noise and sound pollutants and all expressions of visual content are digested in one form or another via our *consciousness*. Subsequently remaining still and at that grounded place is hard. Digital services that play into the overproduction of cortisol and the perpetuation of stress on the brain chemistry, are no longer necessary, nor are they beneficial to you as a designer, or business owner. People, you see, will eventually find themselves sick of it all – and will search out that which contributes only to their inner peace and growing development as a being.

The types of experiences we are talking about are the very ones that build habits. To return to our phone dating analogy, when the phone goes DING, and you think you've hit the jackpot, dynamic change is underway. What follows is a rapid shift in energies, a tightening of the muscles, then perhaps even a shiver of hope. Like Pavlov's dog making a conditioned response, an almost imperceptible shot of excitement spurs you into action, and you follow up the invitation. What is the point, we have to ask, of our sensations, our memories, our cognitive abilities, if these do not lead at some point to action, be it walking, or reaching, or swimming, or eating or even writing? I like to think of them as the gut feelings, and so we may wish to observe ourselves, see where our emotions are pulling us and be mindful of the kinds of responses we make, and then the actions we take. In practising mindfulness, we are taught to be the 'observer' because to observe our emotions and not be governed by them is another way of being objective and finding these triggers interesting as opposed to allowing them to mediate our everyday actions. There are myriad ways in which decisions and behaviours can stray from the axioms of rational choice, and as we observe the new generation evolving in a digital world, we are starting to see the actual effects of this new 'lawnmower man' existence. It starts with a swipe to the left or the right and places a new level of discussion on the age-old concept... of free will.

Tomas Chamorror-Premuzic, a professor of business psychology, writes for The Guardian in an article titled *Virtual love: is your Valentine an avatar?*:

'Many of you will find this idea of digital dating absurd or pathological, but let's not forget that the contemporary notion of relationships as romantic has not always represented the norm – in fact, love, as we define it today, is a fairly recent idea. In the times of the cavemen and primitive tribes, the mate was simply captured. In medieval

times, marriages were engineered for pragmatic rather than emotional reasons, as is still the case today in much of the developing world. More recent rituals, such as random drunken encounters at a bar or club, or online dating, are not always driven by love either and hardly qualify as romantic. The impressive success of digital dating apps is arguably based on its ability to simultaneously cater to our primordial instincts and our postmodern obsession with efficiency.'

We don't think about these very basic, primordial things when we design; we just create a better interface. To the design community, in any new interaction, there are only three dimensions to an interaction: i) the human, ii) the device, and iii) the environment – and we can get smarter at designing these things. Tech just caught up and the device output should now be more intelligent in using the environment to personalise and contextualise the interaction to advise you about your behaviour – and nurture you because, as Elspeth Huxley said, 'Only man is not content to leave things as they are but must always be changing them, and when he has done so, is seldom satisfied with the result'.

People are dynamic creatures with dynamic thoughts, emotions, and psychological forces. To understand people we have to consider all possible factors that influence a person's behaviour and consider how those factors interact and change in time to affect the person's present state. So, in designing solutions that start to move the needle on behaviour and break biases, it's imperative that we look at all the factors and then begin to influence people with only their benefit in mind. That means understanding what those interests are – not deciding that 'this' or 'that' will be good for—them—based on *our* indoctrinations. It would seem that one has to break one's indoctrinations and then re-enter the design process somewhat consciously.

Reversing negative brain patterns and negative cognitive biases start with understanding people – like Erich Fromm says: *gaining knowledge*. It then moves out from there to a series of small interactions. This is what can indeed be considered as being responsible as a designer. Responsible. It is a Greek word and comes from the phrase respond. This means returning to what people need, (gaining that knowledge) and then servicing that need.

Here's an interesting, hypothetical (or is it?) case study. Let's say a social network you use every single day is sitting on top of the large set of data generated by tens-of-millions of people just like you.

The whole system has been designed right from the outset to get you hooked, extracting information such as your location, travel plans, likes and dislikes, status updates (both passive and active). From there, the company can tease out the sentiment of posts, your browsing behaviour, and many other fetishes, habits and quirks. Some of these companies also have permission (that you will grant them access to, in those lengthy terms and conditions forms) to scrape data from other seemingly unrelated apps and services on your phone, too.

One of the social networks you use every day even has a patent to *discreetly* take control of the camera on your phone or laptop to analyse your emotions while you browse. Using all this information, the company can build highly sophisticated and incredibly intricate models that predict your outcomes and reactions, which also include your emotional and even physical states.

Most of these models use your 'actual' data to predict and extrapolate the value of an unseen, not-yet-recorded point from all that data — in short; it can predict if you're going to do something even before you might have decided to do it. The machines are reading our minds using predictive and prescriptive analytics.

A consequence of giving our data away without much thought or due diligence is that we have never really understood its value and power. And, unfortunately for us, most of the companies ingesting our behavioural data only use their models to predict what advert might tempt us to click, or what wording for a headline might resonate because of some long forgotten and repressed memory.

Perhaps all companies bear some responsibility to care for their 'users' data, but do they care for the 'humans' generating that data?

That's the *big* question. Because usernames have faces, and those faces have journeys, and we've spent a long time mapping the user journey or plotting the customer journey when, in reality, every human is on a journey we know nothing about.

Yes, the technical, legal and social barriers are significant. But what about commercial data's potential to improve people's health and mental wellbeing? We can keep letting companies use our data to pad out shiny adverts, or we can force them to use that same data and re-tune the algorithms and models to do more — *to do better things.*

Let's go deeper into that company's data collection and what they could do with it if they wanted to do better things. Suicide. Suicide is a global problem, particularly in men. It's because a significant portion of men never feel like they can talk to anyone about their issues. Because they feel ashamed, do not want to discuss feelings or just 'don't want to make a fuss'. There's a generation of men whose adult lives have been marked by major social changes affecting the workplace and family and they're in pain. They don't have a way of offloading all that stress and inner turmoil that speaking so often releases. Congratulations, the technology we created to smooth out checkout processes and guide people through financial trouble is also able to help these men talk freely. Artificial Intelligence could be the key we need to turn to, to unlock the cure for the silent killers.

Using Artificial Intelligence and Machine Learning, it now seems entirely plausible for us to be able to predict whether people may develop a mental health condition or psychosis by analysing transcripts of their speech. The analytics could focus on telltale verbal tics: short sentences; confusing, frequent use of words like 'this,' 'that,' and 'a'; as well as a muddled sense of meaning from one sentence to the next.

But for many of companies who collect our data, the subject of suicide prevention is too contentious to provide a marketing benefit worth pursuing. They just do not have the staff or psychotherapy expertise, internally, to handle this kind of content. As people, we're used to being served up adverts. Being sold to has been normalised, being saved has not. Which is a shame when so many of these companies would also benefit from keeping their customers alive.

Where the boundaries further get blurred and the water murky is that to save a single life you would likely have to monitor us all. The idea of me monitoring your data makes you feel uneasy because it feels like a violation of your privacy. The modern Panopticon. Surveillance. But think about how those adverts are served up, it's the same technology. Where's the quid pro quo? It's also a minefield for those of us designing these data driven services because that road we go down there will be forks and junctions that old media did not have to meet.

Traditional designers might well find the prospect of thinking in more human-focused ways frightening. Whereas interface designers work happily in apps like InDesign and Adobe Illustrator and in order to finda very human-focused solution to a non-linear design problem they will require vastly different tools and skill sets.

It seems that service designers will have to become well read in science, biology, and psychology to truly create the products that society *needs* because data, not intuition, is about to become a designer's most valuable asset (all things we don't really have to think about when our designs are constrained by screens and narrow thought). Let's, though, have a look at how some of this tech is playing out in the world, what it's done to us culturally—and what we're going to do about it.

4. NARCISSUS, IAD AND THE MEGACITY

'I think a lot of self-importance is a product of fear. And fear, living in sort of an un-self-examined fear-based life, tends to lead to narcissism and self-importance.' Moby

I use the term 'Designed Impacts' a lot. Whether intentional or not, we have created a lot of new behaviours since digital seeped into our daily lives and the consequence of introducing new elements into any eco-system is that that eco-system is artificially updated. That's nature. It's exciting and fascinating, but having an awareness of these factors may help people to create digital touch-points to rethink or reframe some of the approaches. Let us have a look at some of the designed impacts now, and some of the behaviours that have emerged because of them, because to me, it seems that despite tech's potential to help us make connections, and bring us closer together, in housing us inside our screens and simultaneously separating us from our authentic selves, it paradoxically divides us by providing outlets for the non-self, an inauthentic self, and a rapidly evolving narcissistic culture, an age of—entitlement... as opposed, I believe, to the more ideal: age of enlightenment.

Narcissism is a term that originated in Greek mythology when Narcissus fell in love with his image staring into a pool of water. This admiration of one's own physical or mental attributes has not found a better home in our modern world than social media platforms, our collective narcissisms spinning these platforms into our very own tabloid newspapers, ones we all get to feature in as the best most admirable versions of ourselves: for me, myself—and I. Facebook: it is our pool of water that we are staring into, reflecting back at us our *persona*. For Christopher Lasch, historian, social critic and moralist, narcissism is, in fact, the psychological outcome of our lack of power: 'in its pathological form, narcissism originates as a defence against feelings of helpless dependency in early life, which it tries to counter with "blind optimism" and grandiose illusions of personal self-sufficiency.' Know the self, get the power back, and everything we project into these platforms will change, and as such, the form that materialises will also change. Facebook is not the problem; it's what we're loading into it that is.

As exciting as social media has been, I cannot help but feel somewhat disappointed by what it has produced – and what that says about who we have become as people and what we value in a life well lived. Evidently, we are ready to 'save the planet', 'save the children' and the 'rainforests', before standing in front of a mirror and cleansing the self of our narcissisms, habits of self-absorption, of the ego, our psychosis and especially our fears. We want to save the entire planet and the children of Africa while writhing in the cesspit of Facebook profile pictures, and attaching the self to an ideology that fits our narcissisms, and if we can't find it in the West – we travel east. With cheap air travel and more freedoms to work from home, this is after all something that should be our entitlement.

It seems that there is no straying from the self. For designers and consumers, to achieve anything that can be defined as progress, the discussion will need to incorporate the existentialists and the philosophers of old and encourage once again, that mission to 'know-thyself'. To read Albert Camus, and Nietzsche, else, the selfish, entitled age will continue to envelop. Opinions, entitlements, judgements, criticisms, fake rebellions – the Internet – it's a whole space for people to heave into – only to eventually realise that all this effort of winning that argument or uploading that perfect selfie has just cost you half the year…

I spent time with someone whose life had been completely consumed by the Internet. She was eighteen when we met and displayed all the symptoms of someone with Internet Addiction Disorder (IAD). The experience humbled me a lot. She never even knew it was happening until the side effects took over and made dramatic impacts on her life:

"When I was using my mobile at the peak of my problem, it felt like I had a ton of energy and all the little things I was doing felt great, and I didn't want to stop. I was so optimistic about everything. I was also my most creative during Internet usage, researching everything, looking at photos, asking for people's opinions – many of whom I didn't even know. I didn't sleep much. Every morning I would check my phone the minute I woke up, even if I didn't get much sleep the night before. I was all over the place, dominating every online conversation I could find, leaving comments and having opinions. Sometimes, I couldn't keep up with myself. Sometimes I feel like a god. I feel like I can do anything, so my self-worth skyrockets. I can't explain it, but when something trips me up, and that mania burns out, I've got nothing left. No matter what it is—work, hanging out with friends, exercise, etc.—I don't enjoy things because the smallest details annoy me. I think of every possible downside of something, which leaves me dreading the idea of doing anything. I turn into this grumpy person. When I think about the future, I don't like what I see. I can only envision more troubles, endless work, and an endless string of let-downs."

But are the addictions to tech and the Internet a product of digital design or something to emerge out of some more significant ecosystem? A product of a product? Too much time interacting with technology and too little time interacting with humans in the same room appears to lead to some serious social difficulties but is this in fact true? Like the mountain man disappearing into the wilderness, forgetting how to speak and turning mute, we are not practising regularly the thorough conversations with our peers and partners that our parents and grandparents did. Why would we, when we can message through a social media network, or find one of the 128,065,988 answers on Google in 0.47 seconds? It is undoubtedly more polite than interrupting them with a phone call or a visit.

As an industry, we spend an awful lot of time mapping the 'user journey' or plotting the 'customer journey', when in reality, every human being is on a journey we know anything about. How can we? On top of the very personal experiences, we go through during our lives, we also flooded the world with artificial stimulants that take the form of technology.

One phenomenon that has grown out of the modern world was documented when Andrew Marr explored *Megacities*. In the alienating high-tech Tokyo, Marr in fact 'rents a friend'; a new trend to spring out of the megacities disconnected populace and proving that sometimes, there is nowhere lonelier than a crowd. The new symptom of the megacity is not unique to the Japanese metropolis, the rent a friend concept seems to have gone global. Running a search for 'rent a friend' into Google, I find 370,000,000 hits in 0.35 seconds. Once, friendship took time: the effort of smiling in the elevator with that woman you see each morning, and eventually talking about the weather, or on that early morning train or with the man in the café. Friendship was once something that seemed to happen softly, it would grow organically and emerge over time like the plant whose seed you buried months ago, but not anymore – now it can happen—now. Hiring a person by the hour is today not dissimilar to the way we can hire a driver, escort or PA. If renting a 'friend' is not the sign of a collapsed community, disconnect in culture and indifference in our cities – what is? 'Renting a friend because you haven't got a friend is a bizarre, unsettling idea,' Marr states, 'and it says something about a city like this that somebody can be so lonely they have to pay for companionship. It's very sad.'

'Communication leads to community, that is, to understanding, intimacy and mutual valuing,' said the philosopher Rollo May, but if we don't have time, the social skills, the confidence to begin speaking with the person in the elevator, on the train or in the café, and we do have the money and the means to bypass all that difficult noise and go directly to the pleasure that Nozick's Experience Machine is providing, should we not plug in, log on, speed date or rent-a-friend? The desire that the uncomplicated, unchallenging, immediate friendship that the Operating System (OS) in the film *Her* can provide Theodore with within minutes of him logging on is, it seems, all too attractive. Could the rent-a-friend and Internet chat-room phenomenon not forerun this cruel, science fiction reality to next arrive in our megacity consumer wet dream? I hope is that, once again, the answers can be found in the word 'balance', and the 2009 Pew Centre for Internet and American Life survey did reveal those very encouraging facts suggesting that balance is in fact emerging.

So you see, there's enough scientific and anecdotal evidence shining through that shows that for all the positives that the online world creates, there are opposite effects (and this is natural law) and whatever we look for, we tend to find in our research. Being mindful of these results and designing services that factor in those human conditions is more than just good practice, it's the ethical approach to design. While the underlying reasons are yet to be researched in more detail, we can already conclude that digital brings both benefits and risks, all depending on how it is used, as well as how it is understood. But why does this matter? The digital world has not been a failure – in fact quite the opposite, it's the new industrial revolution – right? Moving forward differently is obligatory, and doing so by applying a different approach to design is going to be essential to realising the full benefits of what we can achieve as a species and going to the next level. As a micro example, you may feel like your user centred, empirical approach to design has always worked and does not need to change, which is fine. But what if a competitor applies more human-focused conditions to the design approach?

Airbnb is an active case study of a disruptive business that took a human needs approach to design and is subsequently crushing the traditional players, and every company can learn from this model. It's true that human-focused thinking makes a lot of technical people feel uncomfortable, but there is little doubt that this will have to be our next route in and through the coming decades of technical production.

A human-focused mentality to business is very different from the approach taken by the incumbents. Let us, for example, consider the advertising industry. Marketers working out of their offices rely on years of experience and on customer testing to interpret consumers' so-called interests. They make a plan and design a solution, and the result is this *solution shop* business model. In contrast, some businesses are now taking a different path – by using the human model. Following the protocols of what makes everyone human, and understanding the conditions of living, we are then allowed the space to have a different type of conversation and then zoom in on a small but increasing number of solutions. We're looking at the micro issues directly while keeping a mature handle on the macro trend.

Some businesses I work with are starting to trial a more human-focused approach to projects besides their traditional methods, and this kind of experimentation is something to encourage. Of course, as the results of a product then grow, it may eventually steal people away from those other businesses cores, but that's a good problem to have. Some businesses will try to address the situation before it is a problem – and they shouldn't. Instead, try to flow with it as it is in many ways, the natural propensity or curve that business will evolve forward in the trajectory of.

It then becomes to think of it like this: it's not 'wrong', it's a realignment that is occurring.

It is rare that a technology is an answer to a human problem, it's merely the aid and when new tech is developed, it should never dictate what designers should do. Businesses that focus on the existing model of interface first and feature fixation will become institutionalised in the processes and will thus make it very difficult to make real change. Products and interactions though, that are designed for human benefit, with a central focus on understanding the human condition, will cut through the noise and emerge on the other side as the successors to the day's digital rising. The interlocking features of this as an approach to design may be the key to leading all toward and through this sea change in a way that is in flow, is sustainable, and is in service.

The real benefit of an approach that is in line with knowing who we are and what drives us, and then designing to nurture and care for us as people is that when the interfaces dissolve, human needs continue. Mixing our historic digital evolutionary journey and the innate needs of our mortal state, actual progress and moral value, we can examine the past, present and the future of design and technology in a world that changes at the speed of culture. Then, any of us working in innovation design can articulate in simple terms, not just what problem we are solving, but are then capable of simplifying features—ones that are there for nothing more than only their sake. Ultimately, we translate these interactions into human, sensual, emotive, and functional expressions and this sounds simple, but simplicity is hard. It's all too easy you see – to 'put a touchscreen on it' to check the innovation box. If it is time to lose that touchscreen, what do we lose when we do that? Maybe it's just the fear of losing that touchscreen that is the thing we need to let go of...

5. HUMANS AS SCAREDY-CATS. FEAR OR CBT?

The crowd will see you now, the patient will see you now, Dr Google will see you now, the robot will see you now, the avatar will see you now. Everyone will see you now. Everyone but the doctor.' Dr Eric Topol

How often has fear held you back from doing something you knew in your gut you should—and could? Taking a step back, we might notice that many of our decisions stem from one core fear. What that is will vary between us. It could be a fear of not belonging, of not being the best at something, a fear perhaps of something too challenging or it could be the fear of letting others down. We are all a combination of adapted children, angry teenagers, critical parents, rebellious children and adults and all of these ego states are ones we can channel into – in a millisecond. What moves us between them? What drives us out of the adult/balanced part of the ego? Where we initially feel stable and grounded, peaceful, assertive and in line, only to be shaken and almost zoned into an alternative energetic state? Fear at its core is energy, a vibrational wavelength that is incredibly restrictive: like a straightjacket for our creative flow and the steel bars on the infinite potential we all have as creatives.

When we're designing digital services for audiences we often focus on the apparent attributes; 'does it function well?', 'does it look slick?', 'is it useful and usable?' – but often (if not always) we neglect one of the most important attributes of our planning. 'Will our product address the fears of our audiences and help them past them?' To understand a person's fears—study your own.

Think about a time when you confronted, adapted and learned to overcome a particular fear or anxiety… it was surely empowering and grounding. Now imagine that you digitise that moment and bring it to your audience online. We as designers can, in fact, do this and design this into the solutions we're creating. Creating is the key word here and it is essential for us as designers to realise that we are artists too – artists of a kind. The mind is good at generating doubts and building behaviours that encourage caution. We tell ourselves: 'I'm no artist – I'm just a designer', 'there's no way I'll succeed at that' or 'it's an obvious idea' or 'it's too expensive' and fear has a knack of masquerading as rational thought. Having a big dream or idea is intimidating. 'What if it fails?' 'What if the dream is unachievable?' Often we find ways to reason ourselves out of these kinds of risks – and there is no better place to go to reason out our fears, than those closest to us.

'Creatively blocked friends and family members may find your creative project disturbing,' says Julia Cameron in her seminal work, The Artist's Way. 'Blocked friends may find your recovery disturbing. Your getting unblocked raises the unsettling possibility that they, too, could become unblocked and move into authentic creative risks rather than bench-sitting cynicism.' Much fear of our trapped creativity is due to the fear of the unknown. If I am fully creative as a designer and embracing that which I know and feel to be right, what will it mean? What will happen to me? We have some pretty fantastical notions about what could happen. So rather than find out, we decide to stay stagnant. This is safe, and life will go on after all. Most of these negative vibes come from our negative and fearful friends and family members. Inspired by Cameron's work, 'your enemy within' and the 'commonly held negative beliefs' will encourage the *everyone will hate me* feeling, the *I will go crazy* and the *I will feel bad because I don't deserve to be successful* beliefs – but negative beliefs are beliefs and not facts. The world was never flat, although everyone believed it was at one time. Core negatives keep us scared and, as blocked creators, or entrepreneurs, we sit on the sideline and then critique those who are in the game. Caution is the enemy of our design work, and so we must remember that our intuition is an inner compass that is guiding us and there are obstacles on that road trying to block the seed from progressing up the green fuse, because those obstacles are vibrational, they manifest negatively as worry, anxiety, caution, tension, fear—none of which produces life, or health and well being for the biology of any organ, namely—the brain. It's interesting because it happens so softly. Note the caution, then let it go – and walk in the direction you were going anyway.

You will learn to enjoy the process of being a creative channel and to surrender your need to control the result. You will discover the joy of practising your creativity. The process, not the product, will become your focus. Julia Cameron

Right now, I know this is all uncomfortable because reading this will hit home and encourage an idea down the design path that is currently too terrifying. There are likely inertia and a sense of stickiness, but eventually, it all gets comfortable, and it is easier to write than not write; to design, than not design; to allow a project to flow than to not flow.

Some audiences will talk themselves out of doing something when in fear, and afraid of the thing you're asking them to do – the stuff you need and want them to do – and researchers continue to find evidence that being pro-active and facing fears is the best way to overcome them. But what are the internal processes of perceiving different types of threats and concerns? Fear sends us into a fight-or-flight mode but when we're stressed and not in actual danger, the amygdala can over-fire, leading us to make irrational decisions because it confuses that stress with fear. Neuroscientists do not really understand the pathways through which we consciously and subconsciously interpret fear, but we know about the amygdala and its role in fear and fearlessness, though as with many advances, it appears the more we know about the brain, the less we understand. Going closer to the details seems to always move us further into the unknown. Perhaps the key is to zoom out?

In a study released on January 27, 2013, scientists identified specific neurons linked to a specific type of fear memory held in the amygdala. The study examined how fear responses were learned, controlled, and memorised. It's that fear memory that could be a real killer for your service, and once the service is deemed 'something to fear' an audience will resent it and not return. Neuroscientists have found that a specific class of neurons called SOM+ in a subdivision of the amygdala play an active role in these processes. In another paper published February 3,

2013, from the University of Iowa, we're told that the amygdala is not the only gatekeeper of fear in the human mind. Other regions – the brainstem, diencephalon, or insular cortex can also sense the body's primal inner signals of danger when basic survival is threatened, so fear is a complicated thing, and the biological reactions to fear are powerful deterrents from your product.

In short – when we're faced with stress, the part of the brain that takes over (the part that reacts the most) is the circuitry that was originally designed to manage *danger*. Therefore, it is essential to understand that the impulses that come to us when we're under stress – if we get hijacked by it – are likely to lead a person/the audience astray—or send them off in the opposite direction entirely. Designing the best experiences in the world would still be wasted energy if we were to ignore the reality – that a topic might be stressful and therefore, something to be scared of. Humans display freezing, and risk-assessment behaviours in response to fearful situations and understanding how to switch an audience from a passive to a more active fear coping strategy are key to adapting to the stress and unpredictability of modern life. It's also something we need to design *for*.

Another thing to remember is that it's often the moments of unpredictability that people regret most when they look back on experiences. There's a pattern that we see when it comes to regrets, and that is this: people regret what they did not do—more than that which they did. Fear will make you run and hide, it can motivate you to take action, and it can freeze you dead in your tracks, which in the case of a lot of things we design can mean that services are just ignored or overlooked entirely. But can we consciously condition our audience to be more active and less passive in the face of the fears they are dealing with? For example, debt and financial management online, which is something quite terrifying and stress-inducing for a lot of us. I believe the answer is yes and I define 'functional anxiety' as that moment when anxiety and fear are so overwhelming that they can start to negatively impact a person's ability or desire to face a fear head on.

One of the most common causes of fear is being unable to acknowledge the elephant in the room. When we find ourselves in a situation that is headed south, it seems we'd choose denial than face facts; especially considering that the situation might, in fact, be a good thing. You're in debt, and everything you do to try to fix it just isn't working, but you're surrounded by others who are working hard at it and succeeding. What do you do? These cycles can run for months or even years and in the end – you've made it worse by prolonging not taking control. I believe that we need to start taking a different approach to services like financial management and create experiences that call upon a different set of principles: those used within Cognitive Behavioural Therapy (CBT).

Designing CBT led experiences offers up a way of helping audiences understand the thoughts, feelings and attitudes that influence their behaviours – the ones that prevent better behaviours happening, ones which would allow a person to progress. There's a common misconception that 'tools' will fix a problem but they can't. They can show you the semantic facts, but there needs to be more. Somehow— we need to codify counselling.

The core principle of CBT is to address fears and bad behaviours head on and then find new paths to alter such a course – so in the instance of debt and financial management, often the prospect of receiving honest, brutal feedback is scary enough to spur someone into action. In a lot of cases, fear is so overwhelmingly emotional that people don't take a straight approach to sorting it out. With that in mind, should the core principles of designing services that set out to change behaviour and conquer fear be completely focused on transparency and truth? If systems you see, in their design, were aware that fear was dictating steps in decision-making, it could aid in the caution, nervousness, hesitation of a person behaving in a certain fear-based mode, or not behaving at all. There are numerous options we could choose then to help people in their decision-making: a countdown timer, for example, is fun, encouraging and relatively healthy for people, in contrast with most things of today, things that are becoming more and more distant for people.

It might be that when we notice erratic or even harmful behaviour, we just ask the person what it is that they're struggling with because once we know what that block is, we can start to prepare for those situations before they happen. If you know, for instance, that a person becomes defensive with any reference to their debt because of a fear of (for example) not being the best at budgeting the monthly pay, then we can prepare and serve up features in advance that don't let that fear take over in 'the moment' so as to avoid the creation of a type of self-fulfilling prophecy.

Fear stifles our thinking *and* actions. It creates indecisiveness that results in stagnation and what do you prefer, the stagnant watering hole or the waterfall? How do you feel when you look at the waterfall? Allowing fear to own us is this difference: the one between flow and non-flow. I have known talented people who procrastinate indefinitely rather than risk failure. Lost opportunities cause erosion of confidence, and the downward spiral begins. It is ironic you see then because experiencing our greatest fears is, in fact, the best way to learn what they are and how to cope with them. Going into our fears allows us to understand them and that which we understand is easier to empathise with, and so – into our fears we must dive. Like Neo in The Matrix, we need to *go into our fears*, become them, become Agent Smith and then we can understand them and eventually defeat them, because they were never able to hold anything over us to begin with – we just thought that they were. We gave them our power! Only once we initiate ourselves through this journey do we build a knowledge base that is akin to reason. Until this, we will always struggle to avoid being pulled into our emotions. Lost in the pool of our own feelings, we drown into them and are swept along – and along – and along. 'What just happened?' we ask ourselves.

Like all mythological stories teach, the best way to learn to deal with a fear is for it to happen, and for us to then see that it was not something to fear all along, but rather an experience that we needed to have in order to understand ourselves more (to know thyself). We can spend our lives avoiding the demon, the bogeyman, the thing we fear – but instead, get close to experiencing it or go right into it. It is not then, for us to design financial management tools that will show a person the output of adjusting his behaviours. Instead, show the reality of the situation, and don't encourage the denial mechanisms we all have. Show people their behaviour because else, we are just playing into the problem and as convenient as this might be, the reality is not so comfortable and that which you fear the most *will* come to pass, therefore face it, deal with, go through the experience and exit having learnt. With all of this in mind, it's then really essential as designers that we don't take audiences fears in a given situation as a negative. Fear is a healthy and natural human reaction, as well as what we have said – the thing that leads us closer to knowing ourselves. Understanding and recognising that our audiences have fears and then encouraging them to confront them will help us prevent terror from hijacking situations entirely and owning them, steering them and ruining them, so design your service to be real, don't tiptoe, be assertive – and lead. Knowing the driving fears and understanding that which triggers those concerns will be significant in building for behavioural change that strengthens, so factoring all of this into the planning stages will be key, because then having led a person through their fear, you can observe how they are now efficient in going forward alone, alleviating the workload from your inbox. Having moved through a literal initiation, your customer will remain loyal, because you have led them into the cave to face that which they have been in denial of, and avoiding for months, years, even decades—or a lifetime. This experience for them becomes a meaningful experience, and simply trumps any assurance you could have given them that would have lengthened the problem out.

What is also useful when dealing with people's fears is a clear understanding that at the very least we're focusing on the conditions that do not change – the human ones. Without harnessing and building with these conditions in mind, we will continue to design nothing more than a better version of our current shops or support centres online, designed only around today's constraints, and today's opportunities.

One good example of a more human-focused approach to design is a recent piece of work I did, where bringing the human perspective and fear into the job opened up a different vista of design opportunities. A bank told me that they wanted to lower the number of telephone calls. When we looked at the actual human desires, emotions and needs and turned away from the technical solutions, we discovered that although our client had spent a decade digitising their services, people were still ringing up in their droves for a chat about everyday issues, ones that they could have found the answers to online if they really wanted to self-direct. It's not that they wanted to call, far from it, it's that they were scared to digitise something that they felt needed human intervention. So we designed a conversation instead of an interface. We designed a chat-based system, powered by Natural Language Processing (a subset of *basic* Artificial Intelligence), so our client's customers could talk to them not only about their problems but also about their fears. It's a human-focused technology that works really well in fear-driven interactions.

We'll talk a little bit more in a later chapter about chat-based experiences.

⌘

What kind of factors never change? I have a heuristic formula I've often used to try and frame the challenge of designing in a way that is more focused on people and their environment:

B = f (P,E)

When I started using it, it was the first time I began to pull psychology concepts into my design approach. B = f (P,E) is a principle from something called 'Field Theory' which examines patterns of interaction between the individual and the total field, or environment. It was developed by the Gestalt psychologist Kurt Lewin in the 1940s. Lewin's theory is expressed using the formula B = f (P,E) meaning behaviour (B) is a function of the person (p) and his/her environment (e). This age-old discussion of nature-nurture should never end but connecting the discussion into the field of design means remembering this formula, because Lewin, to me, is the godfather of good design thinking. Born in 1890, he was a German-American psychologist and one of the pioneers of social, organisational and applied psychology. Applied being the operative word. It's important in this context because technologies that excite the mind (such as TV) cannot be a substitute for experience, and hence cannot provide adequate modes of cognitive enhancement. 'Experiential thought' is only possible through active participation in and an engagement with the world. We need to factor in all three parts of the equation to efficiently create the right products rather than continuing to develop flawed ones.

Design hinges on finding a pain point or gap and then creating a solution for it. That's the essence of what good design is and what good design should be. But my design interests have always looked left or right of that core principle. What drives me are the reasons, behaviours and cognitive biases that make someone want to use or not use a piece of design, a service or a pattern, and not necessarily the thing itself. More importantly, I want us all to design products that move the cognitive needle—to drive people back and with that return, allow it to change us in some way, shape or form—often quite literally. One of the major themes in my work, driven out of Lewin's theories, is the idea of a 'life-space' or the amalgamation of all factors influencing a person's behaviour at a given moment in time, not just the screen in front of them. Thus, a life-space includes instantaneous thinking, drivers, memory and intention, as well as a personality within the context of the situation and environmental conditions.

This anthropological discussion within the requirements of design must be incorporated if building for the progress of all is to forward move, and not stagnate within the enclosures of any design zeitgeist.

There have been numerous studies over the decades, looking at the way we evolve and change over the course of our lives. Because our personality touches every aspect of our daily life, it's little wonder then that the study of personality is one of the most significant topics within psychology. Every situation we encounter, every life moment we live in, has an effect on us. It's what gives us our individual personalities and behaviours. Our quirks and fetishes. Our biases and preferences. Behaviourism, as it's often known, suggests that all behaviours are learned, and there are a number of different factors that impact how we acquire our personality and behaviours.

There are also many different phenomena that make us human, and the key is in going after those things, and asking what makes us who we are not what we do. So I'll pose the question now before you go and make a cup of tea and head out for a little walk; *what makes us human?*

6. THE FUNDAMENTAL QUESTIONS

'When I was young, I had to learn the fundamentals of basketball. You can have all the physical ability in the world, but you still have to know the fundamentals.'
Michael Jordan

What makes us people? What makes us human? The great evolutionary puzzle. Anthropologists, psychologists and philosophers have been involved very infrequently in design – an industry that builds bridges between people and outcomes. If one of the things that make us human is to seek answers – to develop knowledge – why not explore these fields? The use of psychology in design is not a novel concept. In reality, we're applying psychology every day since usability is in fact *psychology*. The study of the human mind and the reasons why we do what we do is why psychology has underpinned advertising since the dawn of its rising.

By understanding human psychology, both as individuals and in social groups, by focusing on the ways that human beings adapt and organise their lives around computational technologies, maybe we can start to think of better ways to engage with them. In a world where technology surrounds us, we need a better understanding of how technology can be designed to fill the cracks in our society, rather than create walls.

Problem-solving needs to be built across distributed environments. From Internet-based information systems, sensor-based information networks, to mobile and wearable information tools. That's a lot of interactions. The screens we've designed for are no longer fit for purpose in this world and multi-modal interfaces in which combinations of speech, text, graphics, gesture, movement, touch and sound are used by people and machines to communicate with one another as a social norm needs to be re-organised.

What does it mean to be human in today's world? By answering this, I hope new approaches to design emerge. The language of design could change, and if we acknowledge what makes us human, we might begin to lift our eyes up from our screens and out toward the horizons. As shapers of the future, it is our responsibility to make sure that fundamental human needs are not falling victim to the short-lived fashions of our time.

There are quite a few human languages – Latin and Irish among them – that don't have words for "yes" or "no" – but every language on earth has a word for "why"... Where do ideas come from? What is consciousness? Where is last Thursday? Do they artificially sweeten the delicious glue on the back of envelopes? Once you start asking questions, you become like a five-year-old child. You can't stop... And you become very annoying... What do you believe in? What questions really matter? I think there are only two: "Why are we here?" and "What should we do about it while we are?" John Lloyd

If we were to move from the questions of *why* and the 'what we are' subjects and into the issue of 'which of our characteristics give humanity its unique importance and significance?' we may be able to advance, because this question is not empirical. We've always designed system and digital 'stuff' from empirical perspectives and thus: user has screen; user browses using mouse; user clicks on button, etc. It's a very prosaic way of looking at design. It's very inhuman by the nature of being so empirical. What if instead, we were to focus more on our 'pro-sociality' traits?

There are specific characteristics that define what makes us human and these seem to differentiate us from our closest primate relatives. Psychologists have identified these components, which are observed among our species, and key among them is the tendency to imitate the things we see and hear. This is evidenced in human socialisation and expressed in the art forms. Language is the basis of our learning, beginning with pre-verbal sounds learned as babies and imitated from those who nurture us. Further evidence for human pro-sociality can be seen in the way we react to others around us, by interpreting feelings and emotions and then empathising or even exploiting these insights to our advantage – benefiting from individuals that we encounter by offering help and showing compassion or by defending against perceived and potentially real threats. These positives are balanced by negative consequences of the power to intuit feelings but not all our actions are governed by pro-social learning and intuition.

Mood and emotions play a demonstrable role in determining our behaviours. A sunny day can lighten the mood until we see good in people – instead of conjuring bad through our paranoia and superstitions. Indeed studies have noted that a positive correlation can be observed between being in a good mood and the likelihood that you'll help out a colleagues or neighbour: the 'feel good–do good' phenomenon is as a consequence, something that can be designed in and catered for. Even feelings of guilt often lead to pro-social activity. In a virtuous circle, these pro-social behaviours have a beneficial effect on self-esteem or the way we feel about the situation we're in at the time and they improve mental health – the intrinsic reward of pro-social behaviours making them more likely to occur in the future. Conversely, a correlation can be established with negative feelings such as fear and the absence of pro-social outcomes. Other unique behaviours that are ours and ours alone might give us the clues to designing things in a more human way. Did you know for example, that there are three human behavioural traits not found in any other species? Symbolic behaviour, language, and culture are unique and exemplify what it means to be human.

The importance of symbols in the design world is apparent, but it is essential at this stage to understand why we use symbols and their role in the way that humans attempt to understand the world. Symbolic behaviour enables us to recall events from the past and contextualises them in the light of what we now know. Further, we can extrapolate known situations to create a vision of what the future might be or to imagine alternative outcomes to any given situation. This behaviour that is uniquely human relies on shared symbolic messages, which allows individuals to combat the uncertainty of novel situations.

A social act involves a three-part relationship: an initial gesture from one person, a response to that gesture by another, and a result. The result is what the act means for the communicator.

In the study, Applied Organizational Communication by Harris and Nelson, seven propositions are defined, which, if they are indeed part of what makes us human, start to give people who are designing solutions a more human-focused ground to stand on.

1. Complexity creates a reliance on symbolic messages.
2. Uncertainty promotes a continual process of organising.
3. Symbolic behaviour creates and maintains organisational cultures.
4. Symbols constitute the basis for interpersonal reality.
5. Groups reaffirm the importance of symbolic behaviour.
6. Leadership requires effective symbolic behaviour.
7. Incongruences and paradoxes are managed through acculturation.

Both humans and non-human species communicate the symbolic behaviours outlined, but the defining human characteristic is in the ability to contemplate a range of possible outcomes and plan for each with alternative strategies. This 'theory of mind' is absent in other species, as is the associated behaviour of sharing and communicating such thoughts with others. The ability to share symbols and language about the past, present and future distinguishes humans from other nonhuman primates, and the shared use of symbols leads to us identifying with those who share our values, and needs and this leads to a sense of the individual belonging to a particular group or culture. In a world where global communication is the norm, we now define ourselves as part of a species, as well as the narrower role: that of a tribe or race.

Language can be used to persuade and guise. In the world of advertising, the theory that 'content is king' has rapidly evolved into the need to engage an audience through that most human of activities – storytelling. Through this medium, humans employ a language of familiar patterns and ordinary meanings, which is widely understood – and so, therefore, often requires little explanation. In *The Uses of Enchantment: The Meaning and Importance of Fairy Tales*, we understand the fairy tale as a story, for psychologist Bruno Bettelheim actually exists in that Jungian collective unconscious. Simply placing children in front of fairy tales without trying to explain who is who and what is happening is all we seem to need do, while allowing the story to unfold and for their consciousness to digest. Acting as a form of acupuncture for the unconscious, fairy tale, literature and so on thus require little explanation or interpretation and instead combine an experience that mixes theory of mind and this shared language body we all are somehow able to reach into and access, as if connected to through an invisible wire (a super-computer that we cannot see – the collective unconscious). We really do share a unique form of communication. Understanding language and especially propaganda and the way it can be used to lure and move us in ideology and desire, can be an incredibly powerful position to embrace. As we become less the victim of mixed messages and more grounded in discernment, the less we will play into unethical communication and the more authentic and moral our use of language in conversation and design will then be.

'Who am I?', 'Why am I here?', 'Why do I exist?' These questions have driven us to think, speak... and be. They have formed philosophy as a study, and our cultures. 'Is there a God?', 'What is really real?' and 'What is good or bad?' We are communicating with each other while trying to find answers to these things. Some people claim to know the answers, and we believe them... or at least we want to. We pay corporations a lot of money for responses to these things, to the—*secrets*. The study of the human mind and the reasons why we do what we do is why psychology has indeed underpinned advertising, but don't blame advertising, religions that coerce and the charlatan for selling you the product or the ideology. That would be to pass blame. Don't blame the self either, instead – study the design of language and all will be revealed.

Human beings are not like the other animals. We are able to attempt answering the fundamental *Who am I's*. This helps us lift existential anxieties by talking, painting, writing, singing, taking photographs or making film and as we strive to answer the questions – we communicate with other life forms. Communication is then the lifeblood of our human experience. For Stephen Fry and many others, language holds a much greater and more important totality than just a piece of communication *apparatus criticus*, it actually has the ability to evolve us as a species. Not that we may have realised, as it comes so naturally to us but this 'extraordinarily sophisticated system of communication... uses more brain processing than any single other thing we do, whether it's music or art or chess or mathematics or any other high functioning, high cognitive operation, language is the thing that uses most.'

Humans acquire expertise in using our bodies through physical practice (experiential cognition) and we develop mental models of any situation we encounter through our thought processes (reflective perception). Both are the result of experiences, testing and repetition, selecting behaviours to achieve the desired outcomes. The experiential tends to assume a greater importance for designers in our approach to building interfaces because the changes are observable and their effects are easier to measure.

Revolution is an overused word but we have witnessed a genuine revolution in tech in the last two decades, since I went from scanning in photos of engine parts to creating Artificial Intelligent systems designed to teach people more about themselves than they've ever known. The last twenty years has eclipsed anything since the world became industrialised. Ubiquitous global connectivity changed the information construct, experiences went urban and apps and services proliferated in ways nobody expected. In this new space emerged human behaviours that even scientists could not predict, and are still trying to understand.

I've always approached design by answering an incremental set of questions regarding the relationships that are established between the design artefact and the people. It also taps into the thing that makes us human in this ever-increasing digital world. By designing systems that help us to empathise with a given situation or reflect upon our own role in solving problems, it is then instantly more desirable to people than one that spoon-feeds us the results.

As we build further and connect deeper into the World Wide Web, one observation we can make regarding new behaviours is this: new behaviours are not the property of any one unit of the eco-system, but a feature of the system that seeds the network; one that creates its bio-diverse appearance; one that is needed for it to organise itself as such. It's as if the relationship people are having with the web is in fact creating *it* as much as *it* is creating behaviours. In the same way a spider does not exist without its web creation, it's the same. It has been – for us – a dance we've all been participating in, and like any relationship, both sides seem to—*adjust,* only to then flourish a construct that eventually emerges and uniforms itself into a shape that we recognise, such as – the Internet. This 'emergence' could perhaps be that *Categorial Novum* (new category), as Nicolai Hartmann, one of the first modern philosophers termed it, or a process where larger shapes have arisen due to interactions among micro entities.

As with other organic things, digital collectivises into a self-organising arrangement. Some have seen it—many can now feel it. It's quickly becoming then, the modern day manifestation of that East Asian belief known as the Red String of Fate. According to this myth, the gods tie an invisible red cord around the ankles of those that are destined to meet one another in a certain situation or help each other in a certain way. Might we have fooled ourselves into believing that we're in control of what we've been doing—when in reality, we've created something that is in nature—chaotic? Designing for that chaos, therefore, is almost impossible and so all of the adjustment work and massaging of digital will in fact never be able to truly change people.

Nothing endures but change. There is nothing permanent except change. All is flux, nothing stays still. Heraclitus

The modern Internet was built on the principle that we took those paper things called brochures and chopped them up, pulled out the words and re-uploaded them as pages that could be accessed on machines. We added buttons to those pages so people could buy some of the things they were seeing. Though, if that is the case, the modern Internet is then founded on a slightly flawed principle. We took a behaviour and digitised it, then another and another and another but we're not digitising behaviour… *we're behaving in a digital world.* Here's a crazy thought, perhaps it is time to put some healthy friction back into experiences. For example: how might we design a music streaming experience geared toward our unique ability to appreciate art?

Distractibility, illogical behaviour, and other concurrent characterisations are responses to the rigidity of the way in which computers operate. Those characterisations are related to the way in which technology can impose on people a certain type of behavioural and mental effort (i.e., to pay attention, to speak grammatically, etc.). In addition, the information overload we created produced a feeling of inadequacy in society that became aware of its own intrinsic limitations; such as, the deficiency of the mind to memorise more than a certain amount of information, like passwords and usernames and the incapacity of some generations and demographics to cope with innovation.

We now have the ability to create really intelligent interfaces and behavioural modelling, information visualisation, and adapt content to accommodate different display capabilities, modalities, bandwidth and latency in a way that we never had before. For the first time in history we have technology available to create homogenous platforms that can tailor specific solutions to address the special needs of particular communities, demographics and abilities – an incredible achievement and one that needs to be designed for carefully. When we approach design using more disparate experts from fields such as Ai, game design, and app development, then toss in a human challenge related to a human condition, the output will be so uniquely different that what emerges should be nothing short of—brilliant. It's an uncomfortable way of working, but not because it's wrong, but because it's not what we're used to. Products should morph and evolve and become interconnected over time. Lest we forget – as da Vinci taught, all things are interconnected. Realising this is the great work for us and in embracing this, things will simply 'line-up' and the interconnectedness will be something we are in sync with, and not hiding from. Don't solve problems, but design ideas that trigger the solution to unfold. It's noteworthy that this idea that going deeper to get better results is giving way to the notion that the way to get the most interesting results is to be able to go a bit diagonal.

Throughout our discussion, we have returned to the fundamental questions and observed that since the dawn of humanity, people have asked these questions about themselves: 'What is the meaning of my life?' and 'How do I cope with my mortality?' Greek philosophers as well as leaders of religions have proposed answers to these complex questions. In the 21st century, technology seems to have, at least *partially* replaced the role of the philosophers and the clergy in supporting individuals in their existential search process. This does not need to mean that literature, the study of the epic poems, the creation of fine art works and symphonies needs to dissolve away as tools to access the higher realms of knowledge, but should continue with conviction and commitment. Technology should simply do the same. Put simply, it can effectively support individuals in searching for answers to the fundamental questions. In bridging the gap between it doing this and where we are at now, we first need to develop the schematic and then build into our designs more human support features. To bridge the gap, we need to be thinking more human.

7. THINKING MORE HUMAN BEING

'Mathematical reasoning may be regarded rather schematically as the exercise of a combination of two facilities, which we may call intuition and ingenuity.' Alan Turing

A more human-focused approach to designing products and solutions would drastically change how we think about people and the lives we all live. It helps us to realise that people do not behave, as we believe they do. Even under the microscope of qualitative and quantitative, field and desk research, the results are often an observation of the person's mind-set at a 'moment' in time. Technology gives us the ability to track and observe people over 'periods' of time, much more ethnographically than any other method and also makes more regular observations about them—coupled with behavioural, environmental and other psychological factors. I see two perspectives and approaches to human-focused digital. One is based on intuition, the other—on a systematic approach to identifying the change you want to see.

Most of us aren't at such an advanced level in terms of intuitive abilities. It is therefore more reliable to follow a systematic process as we evolve and culture our own intuition. Then you are not depending only on an individual's currently repressed ability, which is going to be very different in terms of effectiveness from person to person, rather: we are harnessing the collective intuition through systems. Remember that collective unconscious we spoke of earlier? No matter how much you trust your intuition, it's always beneficial to go through this process of scanning the ecosystem, extrapolating the future outcomes, developing models, consulting experts, and creating a vision. Often, this can simply support that which you were initially able to intuit – and there is surely nothing wrong with that.

Moreover, let's not forget that technologies create new social practices, specialisations and knowledge requirements. This then adds a new set of social divides between those who possess the required skills and those who don't. The societal implications of new technologies have become more and more complex with the advent of computational systems. 'If we learn the reasons for and the properties of these various technologies, then maybe we can control the impact,' Don Norman says.

Always start your design approach by mapping out the very basic design pyramid in which the classical rhetorical questions of Quis (who), Quid (what), Quango (when), Quem ad Modum (in what way) and Cur (why) are answered. This interpretation of human-focused digital is based on Maslow's hierarchy, which has its base in scientific facts about human physical, perceptual, cognitive and emotional characteristics: followed by progressively more complex, interactive and sociological considerations.

Human-focused digital should answer a series of questions and answers, ones that cross the entire spectrum: from the physical nature of people's interaction with product, system and service to the—*metaphysical*. Good design is about questions, not functions. Ask yourself then, how you want someone to feel and not how you want someone to behave. Designs whose purpose and characteristics are to answer questions and curiosities which are *feeling* powered, further climb up the psychological and philosophical hierarchical pyramid of information gathering. Designs will then be able to appeal to a wider range *of* people—and they will. Subsequently embedding themselves deeper within people's minds and lives will nurture the potential between the design and a person's potential to pull out of it all that they can. Try creating a product then, which introduces a new meaning into someone's life. It will offer deeper meaning and also move it closer onto the path of being a mass need and in turn, a commercial success.

As 'User Experience' practitioners start to shift away from thinking for users and think more for people, there will still be methods that they use today that will benefit them tomorrow. For instance, a user experience designer today should be spending more time scanning the environment and picking up trends that aren't necessarily what the so-called-user is asking for, but what the user-experience-turned-human designer believes could create a more emotional, human experience.

Take a minute to count the problems you've had to solve today. Most likely, you've chosen what to wear, what to have for breakfast, which route to take to work. Once at work, you took stock of pressing demands and made some decisions about which tasks to tackle first. If you're a manager, you might have had to schedule and attend meetings, possibly negotiate with team members on a proposal, counsel some staff, prepare reports or presentations and you might have had to pitch an idea, all before lunch.

The key organising principle in the brain is to minimise threat and maximise reward. This has implications for problem-solving because when we experience a problem that we need to solve, it activates the same parts of the brain that process threats, which in turn impacts our capacity to think clearly and make good decisions. The threat response is both mentally taxing and deadly to productivity. It also impairs analytical thinking and creative insight. Creativity and problem solving does not involve a single brain region or single side of the brain, it requires all of it as one organ working as one. There is no one location in the human-mind that makes decisions and solves problems (all four lobes are involved and so too are a lot of sub-regions), as well as then the entire organism that makes up the human being. Everything, we must recall, is connected to everything else and although we don't see the connections – this does not mean that they are not there. The entire system is connected, and these relationships are built to self-perfect, refine and solve issues that are otherwise premature with respect to our current state of evolution.

The most basic definition of a problem is 'any given situation that differs from a desired goal'. Go back a thousand years or so and this included issues like finding food in harsh winters, remembering where you left your provisions, making decisions about which way to go, learning, repeating and varying all kinds of complex movements. Problem solving has been crucial during the evolutionary process that created us the way we are. Solving problems is good – it makes us better. So we need to think really hard when we're designing solutions about the way in which they are helping people solve problems. I have a simple principle – everything we create should make people better (because the brain is wired to solve and evolve).

I boil all types of problem solving down to two very simple kinds. We have linear problem solving, including problems that can be solved using a single solution and are usually best solved analytically. An example of a linear problem might be balancing a budget because the outcome should always be the same, regardless of the individual performing the task and their own method. Another example would be using Uber. You want to get home, you pull out your phone, you set your location and your destination and you press a button.

Secondly, there are non-linear problems, which have more than one solution and are solved only with a different kind of thinking. They require non-conscious thoughts to come through and lead, and these are what we might refer to as Insight Problems. These organic problems demand a natural approach and thus differ to the linear analytical obstacles in that they don't have obvious solutions or sequential steps in-built toward 'the' solution. They are 'complex problems' and demand something very different to achieve the goal and because the answers are all pinned to infinite variables: the weather, the ability to dance, read maps, read English, and *everything* else, then prior learning is of little help. Such productive thinking involves insight and these problems demand creativity and the ability to combine information in whole new ways of being. Consequently, these issues have the potential for an infinite number of solutions because each solution will hold within it its own credible solution that is relative.

Practice does make perfect, or edges toward perfection and there is plenty of evidence that bears this out. We develop expertise in linear tasks by their repetition, which creates and strengthens pathways in the brain, even resulting in growth of the part of the brain associated with that activity.

Compared to bus drivers, London taxi drivers have a larger hippocampus in the posterior region of the brain. Why? A bus driver's hippocampus has a specialised role in developing the skill used to navigate routes. The bus drivers' hippocampus will be relatively under-stimulated because they drive the same route day after day. The entire problem solving process, complex or simple – from preparation to incubation to illumination to verification – consists of many interacting cognitive processes (both conscious and unconscious) and emotions.

Complex problems though, need creative solutions, ones that come to us in the form of these insights. When we have an idea, what is not obvious becomes obvious, as if a fog has simply cleared and the vista has appeared. In that moment, nobody can tell us that the vista is not real – we simply realise that they cannot yet see it. More complex tasks are less commonly encountered and therefore solutions aren't readily to hand. Faced with what is at first sight an insurmountable problem, we cast our eyes to the skies and seek inspiration wherever we can find it. The key it seems is to try less, do less, and allow the silence to speak to us. The Eureka moment that is always so spontaneous can be hindered by anxiety as that which is being delivered from the unconscious is suppressed through that state of anxious being. When in that more relaxed zone, the unconscious brain throws aspects of the problem into the mix and, by making new connections, delivers solutions for us to run with.

The unconscious can be thought of as our parents and until we are ready to hear something and connect with it, our parents will keep it from us. However, once the unconscious does reveal more knowledge to our conscious selves, we experience the insight and it is for us to take advantage of the moment. Repressing it back into the unconscious is rather obtuse and a habit of our culture while we 'think' too much and procrastination runs amok. The reason this process is somewhat immature, is because all the unconscious will do is keep providing the insight, until eventually we surf the wave that always wanted to take us to the next level, place, country, relationship. The brain is simply pulling together remotely linked ideas as if playing a game of dot to dot without our knowing, to create solutions to long-standing problems – not something our prefrontal cortex is very good at. Letting go of trying to figure things out and trusting that our brain is doing it anyway, is one of the things we find hardest.

We need to start designing solutions for some of life's big problems (like financial planning) that tap into the power of the non-conscious brain. Setting people a problem or challenge to solve and then actually asking them to walk away from it feels counter-intuitive, but it's a genuine neurological recipe for success.

Sometimes the way to do more is to do less and this is hard to fathom in a society that stresses, encourages speed, progress and especially more progress than another person's—*progress*. Anxiety and stress distract people from their silence and clear thoughts, inhibiting their ability to have and pay attention to *insights*. When we are in stress, even the simplest of decisions – what shirt to wear, whether to shave or not, can become a complicated process. 'I can't think straight' or 'my head is not in the right place for that' are certainly phrases that I have said out loud. When we are in anxiety, we are not in flow and insights (those eureka moments) are muted. A great shame considering they are the exact thing we search for in our anxious hysteria. Insights – those special things – they always occur when our brains are quiet, and activity level is low, so we should aim to design solutions that keep an audience in a positive mood from the very start – don't bamboozle, keep it calm, keep it light. It's what I call 'The Smile Test'. How can you keep someone smiling through an entire process? There's an art to it, and the key is not to encourage more anxiety. Lifting off the seals of stress from people will allow them to ground into that quiet place, insights will come to them, and then that smile, and not one that is short or quick and 'chemical', but the other kind, the one that is constant and present and remains, for a long period, the one that emits an inner glow – the one that has come because you have initiated a lighter, more stress-free ride to allow them to be with their insights—to be with themselves.

Does a product make me smile? If it does, then my brain is going to be on a low-anxiety mode and I'm suddenly primed to start solving problems from that relaxed state. Emotions, you see, are the perfect measurement of human-focused products. In addition to their internal and psychological relevance, emotions have a specific social role and when people experience emotions – they tend to show them. Like laughter and smiling, the feeling of happiness has been proven to enhance social bonds. Laughter – it is a good example of something that has evolved from the 'lay face' expression seen in other primates during their chill out time. These very expressions and positive emotions enhance social relations by producing analogous pleasurable feelings in others. Think of some of your favourite people to be around. It's likely they'll emit this very energy. By rewarding the efforts of others, we can encourage on-going social contact. There are thus, good biological, psychological, and social reasons to presume that using emotions as the measurement of your products success, alongside traditional metrics like sales would be relevant to human happiness and your business problem.

Another good reason to judge your product on how happy it makes people is because happy people might share their good fortune (for example, by being pragmatically helpful or financially generous to others), or change their behaviour towards others (for example, by being nicer or less hostile), or merely exude an emotion that is genuinely contagious. Psychoneuroimmunological mechanisms are also in play, and just being surrounded by happy individuals has beneficial biological effects. It seems that everything Greek philosophers, medicine men and the original herbalists taught us has been on point all along, and that a person's mental state completely influences disease and healing. It is key, therefore, to be in health and well-being so we are then able to design that out. Are we for example, asking our audiences to focus on too many things at once? Try to focus their attention on one thing at a time.

⌘

Overcoming an impasse is achieved only with a shift in perspective – a break in the current mental mode. This is hard for us because it is so normal that we learn from past experiences and then carry that knowledge into current situations to reference – this is how we evolved as a species (learning and applying). That which we have applied before and seen work—we use again. Unfortunately, this also hinders our ability to see things from a different perspective—how ironic because it is *this new perspective*, which is needed to so often—move forward.

One of our greatest challenges in shattering the current state of analytical and critical thought is rationality. To solve anything with insight and creativity, we have to stop focusing on the rational, which is often culturally the less *sensible* but we surely must as focusing on the problem and putting further effort into finding the solution within the confines of analytical focus does not allow the space conducive to having an insight. Critical thought and culturally sensible behaviour with respect to problem solving are controlling as these states of being bring a person back to rationality and a rational approach doesn't fix a problem—it just analyses it.

Embracing data and analysis is, in and of itself, rational. In this fashion, the brain thus constrains our ability to creatively strike a problem away using insight by further cementing a particular perspective or corollary into the analytical, often academic border. Limits, boundaries, margins— none of this opens doors. 'This is the way it is, this is how it's done, this is the right way,' halts and stagnates the en flow of all that is. As an approach, this *rigidity* will perpetually firewall the insight—a powerful almost spiritual sound with an ability to help you see and hear the *different perspectives* emanating from out of the void. It's time for disruption. Pride though, has a way of keeping us confined to the space we are allowing ourselves to reach, both in emotion and mind—it doesn't want us to listen to those insights. Letting go of pride, social norms, conventions, theories, conducts and traditions will allow the self to hear and in turn harness an ability to see and feel the different perspectives. Emergence is thus allowed to blossom, as the path of its growth has been unblocked. On March 1st, 1980, at the Thomas J. Watson Research Centre at IBM in New York, Benoit Mandelbrot saw something—a formula. He had an insight. What he envisioned came to be known as the Mandelbrot set, and a set of complex numbers was now able to animate the emergent nature of our universe. A mathematical visualisation or set of 'fractals' were capable of displaying visually the repeating emergence or natural appearance of all things, including natural phenomena that blossom out of the empty and into— *manifestation,* here in our reality—including in psychoanalytics, thoughts or realisations. From the veins of an oak leaf or the pattern of frost crystals on cold glass to river networks observed from space, the flowering birth of an organism that grows 'out of itself' was now confirmed scientifically as being the rising and emanating pattern that was making itself known and present. It was the thing that Dylan Thomas said when describing creative flow. It was: The force that through the green fuse drives the flower.

Try designing solutions that describe a problem to be solved using metaphors or parallels. For example, stop talking about financial problem solving using money. Instead, create a solution that uses a metaphor because it will switch the fixation on the actual problem, to one that's more creative.

Sometimes if we want to experience creative solutions to long-standing problems, we have to step back so that we can see the bigger picture. Studies show that people are able to solve problems more if they visualise or imagine themselves in the future solving their problem. This promotes a form of stepping back, which produces more creative ideas as the unconscious passes them up to you in no different a way than a conveyor belt functions. All we have to do it seems, is take our foot off of the stop pedal and allow the unconscious conveyor belt to keep delivering through that sacred content that is reaching through to save us from our analytical mind prisons!

Encourage the audience to take a break, and go for a quick walk. While this may be seen as eating into the experience time, we know the process of stopping and not thinking about a problem can quieten the brain (allowing for an insight you may not have otherwise had). In addition, research tells us that it is much easier to take a positive perspective on a challenging situation when we are in a good mood. Negative moods are associated with a narrow focus, sometimes referred to as tunnel vision, sometimes referred to as... pride. When faced with a complex problem, allow your brain to gain some distance from the problem and notice how many more creative ideas bubble to the surface. Consider starting your problem-solving tool by asking people what mood they're in and if the feeling is specified as gloomy, then suggest they come back and try to solve the problem at another time.

'Restructuring' as a term serves to describe the behaviours at work in people when we use novel approaches to problem solving and achieving desired outcomes. We should bear this in mind when designing and consider how a problem is represented in a person's mind. 'How does solving this problem involve a reorganisation or restructuring of this representation?', we may wish to ask.

When you step away from interfaces and meditate over the problems you're trying to solve, connecting humanity and design back together becomes quite an abstract challenge. In a rapidly changing world, the separate disciplines of SEAD (science, engineering, art and design) should more usefully be considered together, as a means to promote problem solving and exploration of possible outcomes.

A human-focused approach affects digital product design in three steps:

1. It changes how we diagnose the problems we're going to fix. For example, when we want to diagnose why people don't have enough money, we may be tempted to conclude that they do not understand the value of money or the effect on their future selves. Human-focused design forces us to consider another possibility: they want to save, they know the benefits, but they simply don't get around to doing it. Saving may just be one of many behaviours, such as exercising or giving to charity, where what we do fails to match up with what we want to do.

2. It shifts up a gear on how we begin to design fixes to problems. In some situations it might suggest that a basic reminder will cause unreasonable effects on behaviour, while in others it might recommend a different approach to offsetting biases toward planning our poor spending, for example.

3. It can completely change how we decide on what the scope of a problem is. We have to convince people that issues that they are overlooking may suddenly become interesting ones to solve – if they choose to see them this way – and we can help there. (For twenty years, we've focused too heavily on access to the 'tool', but that focus needs to shift in recognition that the important problems still remain – even after access to said tool is made easy. How do we make sure that people actually save money rather than just use the tool? That is the question.)

Remember, that when we solve, *we evolve*.

8. PEOPLE LEARN, THOUGHT ARISTOTLE... AND QUESTION, THOUGHT SOCRATES

'All things change; nothing perishes.' Ovid

Designing digital products to focus more on solving human problems is not an approach that is too scientific or too esoteric but the most radical. We can define the basic human condition in terms of the events that formulate the necessities of our existence. Birth, for example, the need to move, grow as an animal, express emotions, aspire, understand and live in conflict, and the hardest of all: being mortal. The human condition has always been a broad study, which continues to be analysed in all areas of work by scientists, philosophers, religious scholars and expressed in art, literature, and even dance. There seems in fact no area of thought, research or expression that doesn't link in some way to the exploration of or the investigation into the human condition. Anthropology, numerology – even scientology, yes, everyone it seems is giving it a real go.

Throughout history, philosophy has been the domain of the thinkers who are most interested in the human state. From René Descartes' declaration of 'I think, therefore I am', positing that humans determine truth by means of reason, right back to Socrates, who is said by Aristotle to have been the initiator of exploration into the human condition. This shared emphasis on the importance of reason remains an influence on those thinking about design today, where usability is a prime consideration and therefore human-focused design is concerned with designing for usability from the outset. By definition, a product that requires deconstruction and modification to become more usable was not meeting this remit from the start. While the majority sees lightweight, frictionless design as the goal, for some there is merit in designing friction into the products.

Design doesn't seek to answer all the great questions of existence. You see, technology is created by humans, whose creativity and ingenuity can't yet be matched, let alone surpassed, so that it still requires human intervention to achieve novel solutions to design problems. Our varied experience, talents and inspirations can't be replicated and indeed we are as yet unable to explain how they come about, though many have tried. Through philosophy, the arts and religion we've explored what it is to be human, to live a good life and what factors, such as nature versus nurture, might modify our behaviours to good or evil ends. Through modern psychological techniques such as cognitive behavioural therapy, we've explored the possibilities of changing the human condition (usually to alleviate the effects of conditions like depression) and the possibility of such modification has long preoccupied philosophers, key amongst whom was Aristotle.

Aristotle believed that as humans we have an innate desire to grow, to evolve and to progress. But this is different to the instant gratification and the frictionless results we grab too often as experiences through speedy digital design. With Aristotle's theory of the 'four causes' that every living thing exhibits or 'causes', we can match those beside a real digital application.

When designing a new system, solution, product or business, start by mapping out the four causes as these explanations – or principles – seek to answer the why question that I have been asking now for twenty years.

Knowing what the why is, we can then grab hold of the process confidently and move forward with it.

1. Matter. This material explanation relates to a change or movement that is brought about by the material – the thing that is changing or moving is made from matter.

2. Form. This is the formal explanation that relates to change or movement that is brought about by the way the changing or moving thing is arranged, its shape or appearance.

3. Effect. This is the efficient or moving explanation that relates to the way an agent or exterior influence works on the change or movement.

4. End. This is an event's final explanation and is the outcome to which it tends, if you like, its destiny or purpose.

In Evolutionary Psychology by Lance Workman and Will Reader an oak tree is made of plant cells (matter), that grew from an acorn (effect), to then exhibit the nature of oak trees (form), and then grows out into a fully mature oak tree (end).

Aristotle taught that 'people are conjugal animals,' in that we are meant to join as a couple when we are an adult to build a house, or eventually a clan, and a small village. We are also 'political animals', in that we are driven to build complexity into communities, divide through labour and law and grow structures to a size that it thus requires the use of human reason. 'People are mimetic animals' in that we love to use our imagination and that we 'enjoy looking at accurate likenesses of things which are themselves painful to see,' and that the 'reason why we enjoy seeing likenesses is that, as we look, we learn and infer what each is, for instance, "that is so and so."' Here, suggesting that as people, we do so passionately desire learning. For Aristotle, it was the head of the capstone – that Holy Grail to reach for in our quest and also the unique thing about humanity – our true gift compared to other animals.

The next solution framing principle I want you to use when thinking about your next design challenge from a human-focused perspective is that it is possible to boil almost all human needs down to their board axis and six key themes. Each of which will help you to decide what kind of design problem you are going to solve and what human need you are going to satisfy, using reason.

The Themes:

1. Understanding, Protection and Creation (people like to learn).
2. Support, Identity and Affection (people like to connect).
3. Leisure, Participation and Freedom (people like to have fun).

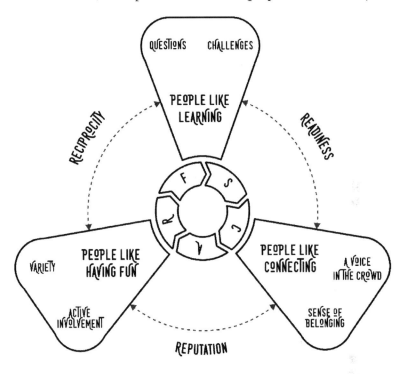

What this gives you right from the outset is a fundamental framework for designing only what is essential. When you focus in on the actual needs of the human condition, what you'll start to create are services and systems that are already more human... by design.

Learning can be defined in many ways, but most psychologists would agree that it is a relatively permanent change in behaviour that results from experience. All people need and want to learn. It 'never exhausts the mind' according to da Vinci, as the continuous learning cycle keeps us evolving as a species but also keeps us satisfied as individuals. So the apparent Uberfication of everything is then a little concerning, to say the least.

People learning in different ways need different methods, but during the first half of the twentieth century, a school of thought known as behaviourism rose to dominate psychology and sought to explain the learning process.

According to behaviourism, there are three major types of learning:

1 - Learning through association - Classical Conditioning
2 - Learning through consequences – Operant Conditioning
3 - Learning through observation - Modelling/Observational

Learning is a change in behaviour or is a potential behaviour that occurs as a result of experience. Learning occurs most rapidly on a schedule of continuous reinforcement, but it is also reasonably easy to extinguish this teaching if we design poorly. In classical conditioning, the behaviour is affected by something that occurs before the reaction. We call it an elicited behaviour. In contrast, the operant response is affected by what happens after the response—that is by its consequences. So what?—you ask.

It is that creating a blend of both is healthy for people. It's how we 'grew up' as a species, but the app culture we create only caters to Classic Conditioning and occasionally Modelling and Observational Learning. That's pretty bad—right? It's important to factor in a good blend of learning techniques into every app you create. The idea of all good designs should be to improve people's overall intelligence, which encompasses using a range of their mental abilities such as reasoning, planning and problem-solving.

Remember when you are designing to consider the following themes:

- Positive Reinforcement. Any stimulus or event that increases the likelihood of the occurrence of a behaviour that it follows.

- Shaping. The method of successive approximations. Shaping reinforces the behaviours as they get closer and closer to the desired response.

- Negative Reinforcement. Anything that increases a behaviour that results in the reinforcer's removal.

- Punishment. Any consequence that decreases the future occurrence of a behaviour that produces it.

When you remove a positive stimulus:

- Extinction. If the stimulus is a reinforcer for the behaviour (e.g., the parent ignores the child/withdraws attention when the child acts up to get attention).

- Response Cost. If the stimulus is not a reinforcer for the behaviour (e.g., the parent takes away the child's TV privileges when the child acts up to get attention).

People all learn in different ways, and there has been much work done over the years to attempt to homogenise us down into archetypes so that designers can create experiences or processes that cater to the bias of a selected group of people. Forrester Research, for example, produced an analysis of six different types of online groups and showed how they could break down the teams by their ages. The theory was that understanding the group can prove valuable for determining what level of engagement an organisation wants to use and for deciding on the best methods to target those demographics.

I have to admit, while broad classifications are used to help boil things down to small sets of truisms, in reality, they're so focused on the supposed engagement behaviours that they then neglect the humanity of the people engaging with a service.

In reality, the experiences that we have with people and in places teach us how to connect to each other and the things around us. It was then inevitable that in the last ten years, we have seen that the technology that has been ingested has also begun to have these effects on people. We've been teaching the brain to react in a certain way (especially when engaged with repetitively) just by the nature of people being 'learners'. We are people. We're not creators, critics or spectators, we're Pete, Merry, Phoebe and Charlie. We learn from technology in the same way we discovered from our parents and everything around us. Too much has been written about creating habits or tricking people into behaving in a certain *way*, I vote we just make technology more human, like us.

I also find it ironic, that more often than not, the focus of a brief is on the business case, the quantitative impact, the qualitative feedback or the transactional push and not the very basic human connections. Observe instead how we're too focused on the goal, rather than the holistic view. We're physical, intellectual, emotional and spiritual beings, not robots clicking through patterns seeking just an outcome. By using distinctions based on the task of the person rather than the human condition of the person, you've automatically started problem-solving with a mechanical motive. When a design is goal based, and not human-focused, we just plough on in making something 'better than the last version of it'. Try though, to remember that great experiences don't attract people and motivate them: they attract already motivated people and inspire them. People are either motivated, or they are not.

When you're starting your design challenge, try to think of interaction more like a first date rather than a primary interaction. You have to stop being so clinical in a world where the technology and the mental model is shifting fundamentally and doing so every few months (but where the emotion of people isn't). Those first few moments of engagement should focus then on the patterns of 'relating' what we learn in infancy and less on the off-the-shelf-design-by-numbers guide to building the best app in the world. Stop studying: start feeling. You were a kid once—remember that.

An expert designer will learn more by looking at psychological attachment theories than by diving straight into the heuristics. Let me try and explain this a little more by exploring what relationships mean (CRM 'experts' lean forward please and learn from a designer). We can reclassify how we engage with people by studying children's behaviours like how, for example, kids are more likely to socialise when their parents are present.

If then, a child is separated from their parents, anxiety smothers them, and they are immediately distressed – until the two are later reunited again.

When you're designing your new shiny service, have you ever considered the anxiety felt by people during your early interactions? Or did you run with the usability manual instead and assume that making it 'easy' and 'simple' would make it sticky? In reality, you could have designed a complicated or even badly considered experience and still made it habitual, just by offering up the metaphorical parent in the room during the first interactions. We've spoken earlier about how anxiety can inhibit learning. Drop the anxiety, and most people will relate to a thing or other person.

Of course, not everyone feels the same way about a given situation. Presented with a new piece of software and asked to engage with it, there are those who will roll up their sleeves and get stuck in – they are happy with what they know, but equally, they are ready for the new experience. They aren't particularly loyal to anything – a designer's dream, you might think. But we should also be designing for the other groups – those who find it hard to let go and tend to remain attached to what they know.

The people who will struggle with letting go of the old system will find themselves to be best motivated by seeing the familiar in this novel experience – and it suddenly wrenching them away from what they know will have a negative effect. Therefore it makes sense to acknowledge the older systems and processes, however flawed the design. This group can be quite demanding and don't have time or patience to learn complicated new things, but once persuaded of the value of your service, they can become your best brand ambassadors and will be happy to spread the word about their positive experiences.

A more extreme version of this would be in reference to those people who will actively resist losing what is familiar and won't be happy to engage with the new service you're presenting to them. They will be unnerved if you remove everything that is familiar and don't see change as a benefit in itself. 'Hold your horses!' they will say, as you offer up your shiny new interface for their pleasure. 'Where's my old one? I liked that, and it worked!' A subtler introduction is needed for these people because they are the ones that will complain the loudest if you get your design wrong. For them, a gradual transition from the old to the new is ideal, keeping them loyal to you while you gently move them away from the past.

If we wanted, we could subject these three different types of early relationship patterns in people through what I call S.A.R.A:

1. Secure People
2. Anxious-Resistant People
3. People who are Avoiders

Recognising who you are working with and for will help you to focus in on and factor in the qualities of such people when you're starting to work on your solution.

Another interesting way of thinking about people and what makes them tick came from a man called David Rock. He developed something called SCARF theory. The model that he describes in his article, *Your Brain at Work*, proposes that the first motivation of social interaction is to minimise threats and maximise rewards—also known as fight or flight. The second motivation for social interaction comes from drawing upon the same neural networks that regulate our primary survival needs. He concludes that the human need for social interaction is as necessary as that for food and water. SCARF defines five domains of experience that activate strong threats and rewards in the brain, thus influencing a wide range of human behaviours.

The brain is focused on increasing or sustaining reward and avoiding negative experiences so ask then if your product fulfils these identified human needs. Are you creating something sufficiently endowed with the right triggers to make it a success?

According to the SCARF theory, the brain continually hunts for five key things:

1. Status – our importance relative to others
2. Certainty – the ability to predict the future
3. Autonomy – having a sense of control over events
4. Relatedness – feeling a sense of being safe with others
5. Fairness – the perception of fair exchanges between people

There are two fundamental positions as far as the brain is concerned – either something is rewarding, or it is a threat. The threat might be something that endangers your life or wellbeing, or it could be something that damages self-esteem – the brain treats the two in the same way. Similarly, the reward position can be a financial reward or something more abstract, such as is: the idea or sense of fair exchange and 'rightness'.

People like to believe that they have choices, and the brain reacts physically to indicate a positive reaction to situations (or cues) that suggest an individual will be able to make a decision. By choosing to break a long-established habit – using an old system or making the same choices – a person gets a sense of pleasure and this intrinsic reward helps to develop the decision as the new habit, making similar decisions more likely in the future. This is what we're aiming for in designing new systems and services – a situation where the individual feels in control and takes pleasure from deciding to make the leap from the old to the new and then for that to be their preferred choice in the future.

Behavioural change algorithms are going to work and be widely available over the next few years, but you still have to teach them what the status quo is in order for them to work their magic. That's the tough part. However, once they know what 'normal' looks like, they can help automate, intelligently, the adjustments that we want to create on/with/for the person at the other end of the experience. Let's look at the shape of a habit, its three components and The Habit Loop according to Charles Duhigg in the three stages of:

1. A cue or a trigger for an automatic behaviour to start
2. A routine – the behaviour itself
3. A reward, which is how our brain learns to remember this pattern for the future

The habit loop is derived from the very nature of habits: that they are unconscious, habitual activities that people engage in without conscious thought. In order to change a habit, we need to explore these three components, use Socratic questioning to get to the root of people's attitudes and know how habits have formed. We might amass data and shine lights into the corners of what might have influenced the original decision-making process from which the patterns stemmed – possibly a long time ago. Another way of thinking about formed habits is in reference to our personalities and our conditioning, something that happened to us from day one. Primarily we are talking about re-learning or unlearning and if you want to re-learn things that are quite big, like for example, a propensity toward passivism or alcoholism, or even anger management, we have to rebuild the foundations. But the problem is all too often, that there is so much choice now, people don't even know what they want or where to begin, and so they wait to see what 'happens'.

If we think of life as a piece of land for example, and even though you have that piece of land, you still don't know what you want, which is fine – because you are waiting, but other people come along—and start building upon your land (onto and into your life), and you have to fend them off, but it's too tiring so you give in to it all, and you say that this is what has 'happened'. You are then lost in the environment of the 'everything', pulled into a million directions. All directions apart from the one you wanted to go in. You may have been rather happy with nothing on your land, nothing but a field, or you may, in fact, wish for 'all to enter' and for some expression of natural order to fall into alignment and for a rhythm to emerge within that – and this may be what you want, which is absolutely incredible and correct for you, as long as it is what you want. Knowing who you are and what you want is the first key (know thyself), because then if things start 'happening', you are grounded in a position of 'choice' where you can choose to allow 'this' and 'that' to happen to you, with you, for you. I believe that until this order or knowing what you want and then unpicking habits down to the bones of the self remain, and for you to build the habits you want in, then life will only ever be a cyclical repetition of undoing bad-habits or in my analogy, a full-time-job fending people off your keep.

If we look at an undesirable habit, the person carrying it out is likely to be aware that it needs to be changed and be willing to make the change. How can we help them? The most successful approach is to improve the behaviour that is triggered, and this is the hardest of all for designers.

Asked why they behave in a particular way, many people will experience a sense of relief that they have this opportunity – it is intrinsically rewarding. This approach is more successful than merely demonstrating to the person the error of their ways. Exploring the triggers in greater detail – when, where and under what circumstances the habitual activity begins – gives the person an understanding and control over the habit. They know to anticipate it, and over time, they can be helped to introduce an alternative behaviour. An example could be the habit of biting your nails, at home in front of the telly, when your hands are otherwise unoccupied. By introducing a compensatory behaviour, to be used in the evenings, at home in front of the telly, we can then teach the person to break the undesirable habit. The new behaviour might be playing with a set of worry beads, taking the dog for a walk or knitting. Thus, the response is modified, but the cues and rewards stay the same.

The new behaviour should be reinforced with the introduction of an additional reward – say nail varnish, or a trip to the cinema in the example above – while continuing the recording of data. Eventually, it is hoped that the replacement activity becomes more of a habit than the original, undesirable behaviour. The key was in giving the person an awareness of what was causing the habit in the first place. We can use the same technique to design technology that can help people to overcome their addictions using the same Habit Loop. If you identify the cues and rewards, you can change the routine.

⌘

I've talked about Socrates. For me, he was more than a philosopher; he was a great innovator too. One of the great legacies of Socrates was his ability to ask questions. He formalised some of his methodologies, and we still use Socratic questioning today and encourage others to do so.

Think of it merely as a line of questioning that probes or an approach that zooms in further to explore the complexity of things, to get to the truth of things, and to open up issues and problems to help distinguish what we know from what we don't. It is systematic, disciplined, and broad and usually focuses on fundamental concepts, principles and theories. In many ways, it is the opposite of stepping back and zooming out, the flip side to that distance away from a problem that's needed to be able to bring *insight*. It is then for us to discern independently when to use such a technique and when to save it for problems that are fitting to what it can deliver. Having gained currency as a concept, this line of questioning is now in use through schools and extensively in psychotherapy.

As the Mandelbrot set helps us see, zooming in and zooming out of the fractal demonstrates repetition, the most uncomplicated calculation for animating the set being the 'escape time' algorithm where the repeating calculation demonstrates repeated detail on a region of the set being zoomed in on or out from and because boundaries within the visual are also pinned to the same algorithm, the self-similarity in the entire visual applies. It is to say 'revealing something when zooming in to and/or zooming out of', (the same thing in its nature, but different in experience). Ultimately, it becomes erroneous whether we choose to zoom in or out of a fractal, as that which is being expressed is the same. It becomes for us to determine whether to pan in or step away from what we are looking at, and neither is right, neither is wrong because we can understand that which we are exploring with a different *approach*.

By employing Socratic questioning in the context of design, we are able to explore complex issues and arrive at understanding the thought processes and drivers of activities that relate to any changes we want to make. By employing systematic questioning and determining a person's knowledge and attitudes, we can design systems that enable them to develop as a person.

This, in turn, leads to systems that are valid and are much more likely to be used by those for whom we designed them.

In design, we can use Socratic questioning in these two ways:

1. For designers: to deeply probe your design thinking and get into the minds of the people using the product. This can help you begin to distinguish what you know or understand from what you do not see or understand (and to help you develop intellectual humility in the process).

2. In the interactions with the person at the other end of your design. Use it in your interfaces (be that natural language or traditional GUI) to foster people's abilities to ask and answer Socratic questions themselves. If we help people acquire the powerful tools of Socratic dialogue, they can use these tools in everyday life.

Designing the questions is an art in itself and merits close attention, in addition to the skills of a professional copywriter – someone whose bread and butter involves the structure of language and dialogue.

Personality comes from tropes and archetypes and personality comes from individual quirks. Therefore having the right characteristics in your work is crucial. Personality design is a lot more than voice. Many studies claim that a minority of our communication is conveyed via words. Messages are communicated multimodally: 7% via words, 38% via vocal elements and 55% via nonverbal elements.

We spend a great deal of time and energy perfecting the appearance of an interface, paying attention to the optimum colour choices and graphics. I advocate placing equal weight on the development of appropriate written content. A critical part of designing the product journey is to understand what instructions they need, and what language will best communicate this information. Teaming up with a copywriter who instinctively anticipates and writes for their audience is the key to designing a successful interface.

In a counterintuitive twist of fate, the removal of all of the artifice actually opens up the opportunity for a more personalised experience too.

I cannot emphasise enough the importance of infusing personality into your design and product. Not brand traits or experience principles, I mean actual personality. If your product were a person, what would the personality traits of that person be? Think about your closest friend/s and base your design on the one that you think would best be able to solve the challenge you are trying to solve. How do they change people's lives? What do *they* stand for? What things do they hate? Are they Bacon or Bread?

One approach I've taken in past projects, against conventional wisdom, is to go and sit in the canteens and staff breakout areas, away from the 'day-job zones and desks'. Then, just chat to the people on the front-line as they come for a cuppa. People who actually perform the tasks and roles day in and day out. Once you've had a good chinwag with enough people, from all backgrounds, roles, genders and walks of life, one or two of them will automagically bubble up in your consciousness as people whom it would be great to base codified personalities on. It's not rocket-science; it's just meeting people and feeling a connection to some of them.

When the overdesigned interfaces evaporate, and conversational interfaces do become one of the primary methods of engaging with people in the digital space, choosing the personality will be crucial to success. Imbue every design with the traits of the person you want it to be and make sure you are thinking about MVP as **Minimum Viable Personality** and not Minimum Viable Product.

When the conversation *is* the interface, suddenly the job is all about crafting the right words. So ask yourself, what *is* the **Minimum Viable Personality** for your digital product? Stop thinking about functions and start focusing on traits, quirks and idiosyncrasies.

Products have features and functions. Personalities have reliability and warmth and depth. So the familiar design patterns we used to lean on when making an app or a website don't work in a conversation-driven interface. As visual design is demoted in favour of words, what you say and how you say it become more crucial than ever.

But beware, one of the first mistakes designers often make as they try to humanise technology is to pursue literal expressions of human features – human body/face, human sounding voice and human-like personality. It turns out that mimicking human characteristics can often have the unintended effect of alienating us. Instead of imitation or replication, relatability turns out to be a superior yardstick for making conversational technology feel human.

A smart phone has an endearing quality to it in part due to the dependency we place upon it and the intimate place it holds in our daily lives. Yet, it does not look or pretend to be a human being.

I don't believe that a machine will ever actually form its own personality, that's pure science fiction. But, I do think that something like artificial intelligence can be deliberately trained with humanistic traits and anthropomorphic tropes, in the language it spews back at us. But it will never spontaneously develop human emotions for no purpose whatsoever, as portrayed in fiction. The control is in our hands to define and code these things.

What is the Minimum Viable Personality of your product?

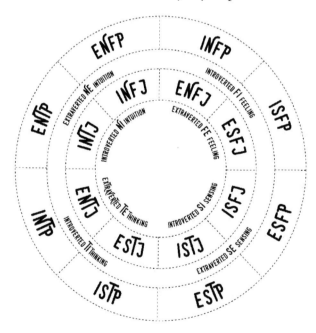

Our aim is always to use simple language that is enabling – and is not a barrier to successful use, as might be the case if we sling in the kind of jargon and technical language that we're used to being asked to engage with. Make it a rule that you gain an alternative perspective by working with copywriters because – like our audience – engineer speak isn't their first language. When you think about it, it's evident that we should use the best person for the job because 'English is hard, but it can be understood through tough, thorough thought though,' said someone.

Youngme Moon and Clifford Nass propose that humans are *emotionally, intellectually and physiologically biased toward social activity, and so when presented with even little social cues, deeply-infused human responses are triggered automatically*. A human-focused approach to digital means attempting to make interfaces more comfortable to use, by leveraging elements of anthropomorphism as the *language* of human-computer interaction.

Since making inferences requires cognitive effort, anthropomorphic language and traits are likely to be more successful when certain aspects of a person and their environment are correct. Psychologist Adam Waytz and his colleagues created a Three-Factor Theory of Anthropomorphism to describe these elements and predict when people are most likely to react well to a designed service. The three factors are:

1. Elicited agent knowledge or the amount of prior knowledge held about something and the extent to which that knowledge is called to mind.
2. Effectance, or the drive and motivation to interact with and understand one's environment (remember my earlier references to Lewins Personality Theory?).
3. Sociality, the need to establish social connections.

When elicited agent knowledge is low, and effectance (a tendency to explore, and influence one's environment) and sociality are high, people are more likely to accept something with humanistic traits. Various dispositional, situational, developmental, and cultural variables can affect these three factors, such as the need for cognition, social disconnection, cultural ideologies, uncertainty avoidance, etc. But don't let that stop you trying to create a good personality for your work and move away from clicks and buttons.

We can also make language work for us in the world of design, by carefully constructing Socratic questions to explore our thinking about a project. You might wonder why we need to make life so difficult for ourselves, as designers – why aren't we aiming for the frictionless approach? The answer is that by thinking critically, we consider all possible outcomes and strive for the best possible outcome. We need to be asking, not just the obvious questions, but the ones that help us to delve into how people feel, what assumptions they are making, what evidence they base their decisions on and what alternatives they have considered. Designers should ask questions but also ask each other why the issues are relevant – this metacognition leads to exploring whole new avenues, and hopefully considerations of options that hadn't immediately presented themselves at first.

The same in-depth questioning process can be used to investigate the motivation and attitudes of the consumer of your design. You'll hope to learn about the extent to which they will put up with change, and unexpected outcomes. By examining a variety of feedbacks, including the respondents' best guess about how others might feel, we build a comprehensive picture. This methodical approach is slower but more thorough than opting for what the consumer says they want or what the designer thinks they need at first guess.

9. PEOPLE LIKE TO CONNECT (AND BE HAPPY)

'Learn how to see. Realise that everything connects to everything else.' Leonardo da Vinci

Being social is a fundamental object of human existence. Designs therefore that have sociality laced into them are more likely to resonate with people and drive more significant commitment.

Despite using all this brilliant technology, it appears that people still aspire to increase their human-to-human connections. In a recent study it was verified that over seventy-five percent of the respondents wanted to attend more live events than ever. So perhaps technology is driving us to be more connected by virtual means, but as humans we still seek the social interaction. This desire might not be borne out in reality; however, as figures suggest, we rely more and more on technology to keep in touch with those we know and those we don't: strangers. Whether we realise it or not, technology plays a huge role in satisfying our need to communicate with our peers and brands can and do exploit this to market their products and services to us where we spend our time.

Emotional states can be transferred directly from one individual to another by mimicry and emotional contagion; people can 'catch' emotional states they observe in others. We have an ingrained sense of belonging as people and therefore feed off the conversations, content and knowledge we share. We also inherit good and bad emotions from other people through a process of entrainment. In the same way one hundred out of time clicking clocks would eventually all sync through entrainment, people are no different, we all align together as iron filings as if constantly self-arranging in accord with an invisible power magnet. In a test at a university in the U.S., students randomly assigned to a mildly depressed room-mate became increasingly depressed over a three month period, and the possibility of emotional contagion between strangers, and even those in ephemeral contact, has been documented by the effects of 'service with a smile' on customer satisfaction and tipping. As if able to ripple out, moods of anger and/or happiness seem to have this effect. With the invention of the telephone, this was suddenly something we could do to and with each other over long distances – affect another person's emotional state. With this in mind, the power of the Internet is colossal.

Scientific studies have shown that the effect individuals have on the positive or negative mood of their neighbours can be measured. The chances of a person being happy if they are in close proximity to a happy person is greater than it might be just by chance. This positive correlation is mirrored when the opposite scenario is examined: an unhappy person can be shown to have an adverse effect on the mood of those around them. Further, the effect on a person's mood is shown to be greater the more closely the 'influencer' is connected to them. What the study goes on to prove is that people who are more socially 'one degree' connected to people are happier and that happiness spreads through a network – and even in digital space. So when designing in social to your service, don't just assume at the basic functional level that you create a button to share or a forum or a like button and that equals 'social'. It doesn't.

At the core of social are three core types of proposition:

1. Induction, whereby a simple viral mechanism is used to pass information from one person to another. This can also be a sentiment or feeling or emotion.

2. Homophile, whereby individuals choose one another as friends and become connected. In this instance the tendency is that like attracts like.

3. Confounding, whereby connected individuals jointly experience contemporaneous exposures — common goals bring people together — more like living in the same neighbourhood.

Designing frameworks that play explicitly to one of those three structures is crucial. While there are many determinants of social feelings and happiness, the social effect is apparent and whether an individual is happy also depends on whether others in that person's social network are or were happy.

In many studies, it is observed that the really happy people tend to be located in the centres of the *social networks* and in large clusters of other happy people. It's not that shocking then, that happy people attract more joy. I love this idea—that the happiness of a person is associated with the collective of people up to three degrees removed. In other words, happiness is not merely a function of individual experience or individual choice. Changes in individual happiness ripple through social networks and generate large-scale changes throughout. These effects can be thought of as being effects *of* effects and subsequently don't need to be limited to the observed three degrees, but instead have the potential to lead toward total sea change in culture. In this sense, we are more like ants than we realise, an interconnected cultural eco-system communicating through invisible chemicals and that means this: if you have a vocal, happy customer sitting right in the centre of your feedback loop—keep them happy!

The pleasure we gain from positive experiences is such that we can't help but want to share them. This altruistic behaviour stems from feelings of empathy for the recipient of our largesse and these are more likely to occur, the closer we are to the person. Such pro-social activities are most remarkable when the benefactor and beneficiary are entirely unknown to each other; when, for example, a Good Samaritan crosses the road to assist a stranger who has been ignored by other passers by. Physical interaction isn't possible in the digital world but the good news is that people tend to be more social and helpful. So, by designing in the opportunity for people to be social with other people, or with a system deemed to be humanistic, we have the real opportunity to create lasting connections.

Baking in social is not as straightforward as most designers would have you believe. A lot of people think 'being social' is merely the act of adding a Tweet This button or a Facebook 'Like'. However, in reality encouraging social behaviours is more non-linear. You must help the person using your digital product to indeed exert what makes them a person by allowing them to i) Assess, ii) Realise it as a thing they add value to, iii) Respond and develop responsibility and iv) Become active.

As with offline situations, people are most inclined to help those they identify with in some way: members of the same self-selecting group are more likely to elicit a helpful pro-social response because their peers feel closer to them and more emotionally engaged and therefore in some way responsible for their welfare.

Of course, everyone is different. Whether or not an individual responds in a pro-social way has been shown in studies to depend on what is healthy for them – we're all predictable. If we think that it is morally right to give to charity, for example, and we do so without pressures from others or with hopes of rewards, we will be more disposed to help in any given situation. We do it because it feels right and our feelings of compassion are rewarded by feelings of satisfaction and by gratitude from the recipient. Of course, our personal moral position is often guided by what is the social norm in our peer group and reinforced by their approval or disapprobation for our actions. In general, those who are disposed to carry out empathetic action are seen as being agreeable, responsible individuals, emotionally well adjusted and connected to others in their group. So the emotional state of the donor and the reaction of the recipient, as well as the group as a whole, can be seen to have significant bearing on the likelihood that an individual will behave in a pro-social way. So when something completely unexpected and awesome happens to them online, the chances are they will want to share it – this is what we are designing for – the ephemeral moment of vitality that stems from known pro-social behaviours.

Directly related to this idea of happiness and human behaviour, is the way I always reframe any design challenge to make them instantly more human by approach. Whilst being aware of the social aspect of any task, I am also mindful of the implicit nature of the task too. It not only helps to create more empathy with the challenge, it drastically simplifies it.

When any new brief comes in or I want to design something entirely new and ad-hoc from scratch, I always start by categorising the function or feature into one of four broad, human focused dream categories. This helps to identify the nature of the task and, by doing so, we can also see how function or feature might morph from one type to another over time. This can be done with anything and everything. Legal cases. Interface challenges. Life goals—anything.

The other exciting thing I've spotted is that some designers are significantly better at one type of design challenge than another. It's like they're hardwired to think in a particular way. You might then, be able to use these four groups to plan your team dynamics as well as design the outputs.

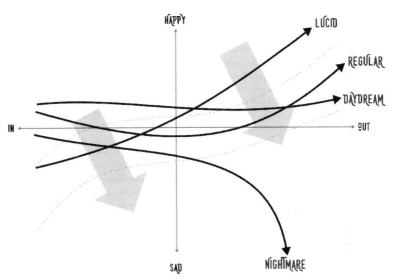

Day Dream Tasks

Studies reveal that the average person daydreams seventy minutes of their waking day. People enter a type of hypnotic trance, switching off from reality for their unconscious thoughts to then rise to the surface. During daydreams, people are semi-awake. They're apparently not asleep, but not fully checked-in with reality either. A daydream starts with a compelling thought, memory or fantasy, and the imagination runs away, which is not unlike a lot of digital interactions that we see. So Day Dream designs are the things that become second nature to people whether you mean them to or not. It's the sort of activity that people will do almost unconsciously to complete a task – something that's been done so many times before, that they even tend do it while multi-tasking. For example: listening to music or checking social media while making only a minimum amount of errors. Email checking applications are a good example of Day Dream designs as people now use them on their phones between train and office: important time-filling tasks that fill in the gaps. The thing about Day Dream designs is that when people engage in them, their creative brain becomes dominant and they have less awareness of their physical reality. We tend to find ourselves 'in the groove' and doing our admin jobs. Sometimes deeper worries or concerns will surface from the unconscious mind during Day Dream tasks, so it's important you design in some off ramps to the task all the way through the experience (email, save draft, for example!). Focus a lot of your attention on the copy in a Day Dream design, because that will serve to quash any negative beliefs about the future or bad memories of the past. Previous errors have a habit of resurfacing during Day Dreams because when someone is in the zone, past misdemeanours will all too often pop out of the subconscious brain.

Conversely, Day Dreams are perfect for rehearsing positive outcomes too. Someone may envision finishing a task before they've started it, or recall an essential part of the experience before it's reached. Because people use the unconscious parts of the brain to visualise all sorts of *goals*, the same will happen in the subtle, average, mundane UX flows. Day Dream designs can be psychologically beneficial for people, helping them temporarily escape the demands of reality, release frustrations, and visualise a better future.

Regular Dream Tasks

These are your bog standard tasks where you have no idea what's going to happen until you get to them, while at the same time – it's all too familiar. In a typical Regular Dream pattern, you could be doing something entirely out of the ordinary and think nothing of it, because you accept a Regular Dream reality as it is. It is something that just needs to be done. They are actions such as submitting a form or buying something online and browsing news. It is considered, focused, but not out of the ordinary. Everybody encounters Regular Dream patterns every single day, and they arise out of the things you consume all the time – and are essential to the survival of most businesses. In fact, a lot of industries would die without them. Assuming people are sitting in front of screens for five hours a day, you can guarantee they'll do some Regular Dream tasks for at least one hundred minutes. They can be described as the bedrock of all good experiences.

From a data point of view, Regular Dream experiences also offer up great insights into the behaviour of the person performing the task. I call it the second conscious self because people behave in a set way and consciously. It's the best common, passive observation you can take from people. These insights are based on people's thoughts and experiences. Motivation during Regular Dream experiences is usually very conscious and deliberate, which is also why useful insights can be gleaned from them. It is critical that we try to make Regular Dream patterns fresh and alert experiences. You can significantly boost your odds of a successful outcome, by designing bumps in the experiences that get the person into the mental habit of checking whether they're concentrating or whether they've slipped into Day Dream mode.

Lucid Dream Tasks

Lucid Dream experiences are the best types to design for people. From a creative person's position, they're also the most fun to work on. They are rich and immersive, and you can guide people through them into infinite and beautiful worlds of your choosing. Lucid Dreams are the ultimate freedom and are often linked to engaging experiences like apps or games. But what defines a Lucid Dream experience? It's any experience in which a person knows that they're in total control over the entire input and output. Sometimes they can even control aspects of the experience – like the rules or the plot. People can then fill in a lot of the details on their own. These are the moments of total clarity and engagement. These are the marketing moments, the creative adventures. Situations where brands must design to keep themselves at the front of the mind of the consumers they are trying to court.

The significant risk in Lucid Dream experiences though is when something jolts the audience out of the immersion before they're done – like a false awakening. If a reality check is forced upon someone during a Lucid Dream experience… then the moment is shattered, and then the risk is, it will never feel the same again and so starts to feel like a Regular Dream experience after that. The novelty has gone. To avoid this derailing moment, encourage the person to think about their environment before they start.

Nightmare Tasks

This is the one nobody wants to acknowledge or design. Nightmare Tasks are those briefs that are 'the application process' or 'the bad news delivery system.' Some Nightmare Tasks can even be so cruddy that a person's sensory system is triggered and people can feel certain types of pain. Life is full of them, so the best way of defusing a Nightmare Task is to design it so that it engages the audience in a conversation with the source of the fear. In the calm light of lucidity, you can have a meaningful exchange, and that can help explain the cause. Not only does this help people on a conscious level, but can also cancel out future Nightmare moments, as now the issue has been heard. It's key to make Nightmare Tasks very conversational and honest – 'this is going to suck,' you can begin with, 'but let's just crack on with it.'

Classifying any task, experience, design or otherwise, like the four above can help you give more meaning to the work and the approach within context. The goal being: the slaying of all nightmares. But why is context significant? In a study by University College London (UCL), it has been demonstrated that any experience (good or bad), can lead to people carrying forward the said memory in a powerful way—especially the negative ones, while inconveniently keeping only a vague memory of any surrounding context.

Out of that, it seems in our creativity we can strengthen the inaccurate memory we are recalling, which can then gradually chronicle itself within our historical record as being something real—*as real as we make it!*

Hence the philosophical notion that we write our own history and create our reality. This selective archiving happens because the amygdala—the part of the brain used to store emotional memory becomes more active during an adverse event, while the areas that store neutral content such as context can become less active. The hippocampus ("**The Hippo**") is a crucial brain region for forming contextual associations, and it is here, within the Hippo that the research determined reduced activity in those lacking that significant contextual backdrop when recalling the past. People who have suffered especially stressful emotions during experiences can sometimes recall vivid and exaggerated images from it. In improving the health of the Hippo, we can archive our life experience within the real context, as opposed to the nightmare our lacking equilibrium otherwise expresses.

To summarise—put a bit of focus on *eradicating* the Nightmare tasks/scenarios. This will allow space to breathe as you have de-cluttered your internal and external environments from jarring, mechanistic, slightly bizarre tasks such as 'registering', 'logging in', and 'losing your password'. They are painful to people because they are—*just not a human thing*, regardless of how well you've optimised and built them. If you've built a million pound machine for buying things and you've given it the greatest branding, and it's got dancing unicorns and ultimate utility... it might be that all people remember about it is how traumatic it was—to log on.

The Nostalgia: Helping Me To Identify Myself

You're listening to your music on the way to work and a favourite song from twenty years ago starts playing. A fantastic sense of wistfulness overcomes you, evoking fond memories of a friend or a party or a particular holiday. The feeling is bittersweet, though ultimately pleasant. Sound familiar? You've experienced nostalgia. When we recall a previous experience, we have the ability to re-immerse ourselves in that experience, but the way we remember memories is constantly distorted. By recalling a memory of the past, you are remembering it as your brain has chosen to distort it, not by the actuality of its events. When remembering something from our histories, we can vividly re-experience the whole episode in which it occurred - but through a rose-tinted filter.

Nostalgia is an incredibly potent tool for designers because it's a yearning for an idealised past—a longing for a sanitised impression *of* the history. In psychoanalysis it is referred to as screen memory, which is to say that it's not a faithful recreation of the past at all, but rather a combination of many different memories, all integrated together, and in the process – all negative emotions are filtered out. If you can design scenarios that encourage people to look back over previous events, journeys, and moments that they spent engaging with your service – what you'll often find is that the memory only recalls the positives. Nostalgia then isn't about remembering memories at all, and it does not relate to a specific memory, but rather an emotional *state*. We remember the room we were in, the music that was playing, the person we were talking to and what they were saying because of the way it made us feel.

The hippocampus is critical to this process, associating all these different aspects so that the entire event can be retrieved. The hippocampus helps form associations between the various elements of an event allowing one aspect to retrieve all the other aspects: a process known as 'pattern completion'. It's also what enables different types of information to be bound together so that they can be imagined as a coherent event when we want to remember what happened. For example, when remembering who we saw, we often remember other details – like what they were holding and where they were. This means that the entire event can be re-experienced in full. Interestingly, for many years those experiencing extreme nostalgia were diagnosed as being depressed. Indulging in memories of the past was seen as a sign of homesickness and refusal to enjoy the present. It was seen as a lack of commitment to the future with a burdening attachment to the past, but now it's been proven that nostalgia works to counteract unhappiness. The act of reminiscing has been shown to counteract loneliness and anxiety, while also promoting personal interactions. When people speak fondly and lovingly of the past, they also tend to become more hopeful for the future. By recalling the past, they look forward to what's to come. So by deliberately designing moments that encourage nostalgia in your experiences, you not only promote happy memories of previous engagements, you may be contributing to improved mental health.

Nostalgic memories typically entail cherished, personal moments, such as those spent with loved ones. Those memories, in turn, inspire positive feelings of joy, high self-regard, belonging, and a sense of the meaningfulness of life. Nostalgia, then, seems to be one way that people cope with various negative mental states or psychological threats. If you're feeling lonely, if you're feeling like a failure, if you feel like you don't know if your life has any purpose or if what you're doing has any value, you can reach into this reservoir of nostalgic memories and comfort yourself. Give it to your customers, and they'll never curse you for it. So… from time to time, shut your eyes for two minutes and think about the happiest time you can recall—it's good for you.

10. PEOPLE LIKE TO HAVE FUN (AND BE REALLY HAPPY)

'The aim of the wise is not to secure pleasure, but to avoid pain.' Aristotle

People are glued to their screens late into the night and then waking up at dawn and checking their tweets before they've said good morning to their loved ones. We're posting extravagant status updates and self-revealing blog posts – laying our lives out there for the world to judge us. I know people who are conducting deep, connected relationships with people they've never met from continents they've never visited. This is frontier land. We've drenched society in digitally induced chemicals that bestow focus (sometimes a distinct lack of) and new levels of stamina and vigour toward micro-tasks. The motivating engine of the brain firing on more cylinders than ever before.

Why are we so in love with our tech? There are physical reasons – the most fundamental parts of the brain that govern intense emotion and the brains own chemical rewards—dopamine and norephedrine—are in play. Removal of these rewards induces a devastated reaction in us, like the one we see on people's faces when there is no WiFi in the cafe… we may think we can give it up whenever we choose, but that might be because we believe it is just a cultural thing when it is in fact—chemical too.

Go a day without your phone. I dare you. Some of you will start to feel the same sort of emotional pain that you might feel if say, someone broke into your house and stole a lifetime's worth of belongings. But what does that mean if you're going to try and create the next big thing? Let's say you've dreamt up a product that you want people to use every day and you're the kind of entrepreneurial go-getter, then you've got a slight challenge on your hands, because hundreds of thousands of games, productivity tools and other apps are already in the market, and thousands more are launching each week. Many prominent, bold entrepreneurial thinkers are finding that their ideas aren't so unique after all.

Here's a startling fact – 21% of people who download a new app never look at it more than once. All that effort and expense building the perfect product and service only to see over 1 in 5 of them leave before they've even got started. There's another weird anomaly too – even well-heeled companies with big marketing budgets don't always hold sway over the little bedroom developers a lot of the time. The UX is tight, and the research is solid, the app looks good enough to eat and then… nobody uses it. Don't cry, you probably just forgot – the audience is human.

Things are never as simple as they seem. There's a lot more going on than meets the eye. Things you could never have possibly known. Have you ever heard of oxytocin? Also known as, the 'love hormone', it is released by the brain during experiences that are pleasurable. The first of these is when the mother nurses her newborn when oxytocin creates a loving bond between the pair. It is associated with positive emotional outcomes such as empathy and trust, and all these considerations will have a bearing on the success of a design.

There's a risk though: research on oxytocin suggests there is also a dark side to the so-called love hormone because it can increase bonding but also the behaviours of jealousy, envy, and suspicion. When a person's association with an app or service is positive, oxytocin bolsters pro-social behaviours; when the relationship is negative, the hormone increases negative sentiments.

Due to the way the brain releases dopamine, especially during exciting moments, studies show that listening to your favourite music has a similar effect on your brain as other pleasure-inducing activities—like having sex. The precursors to the release of dopamine even respond in *anticipation* of these moments, so there are health benefits to help materialise. If you could get a person to play their favourite song at the same time as downloading and interacting with your new design or service, you are beginning to service your clients in a whole new holistic way.

That new factor alone might give you the edge and stop you being ditched by the 21% of people who download it but never look at it more than once. Novelty can, in fact, help keep a relationship fresh and rewarding. Engaging in the fun, exciting, new experiences even within the same, familiar, experience can get the dopamine and norepinephrine flowing and reward the brain as if it was the first time it was downloaded and the thing felt fresh.

Encourage More Leisure Time

While the brain can seem almost boundless in its potential, it has limitations, such as processing speed, attention limitations, working memory limitations, and sensitivity to interference, which can be both internal and external. When restricted, frustration brews but the designer might have a 'Eureka moment' where the solution seems to present itself to you miraculously. We spoke earlier about the relaxed state in which the ideal solution to a problem might present itself from among a number of possible, but seemingly not all ideal, answers. The problem with Eureka moments is that they can't be made to occur to order.

Eureka can be conceptualised as a two-phase process:

1. The first phase requires the problem solver to come upon an impasse, where they become stuck, and even though they may have seemingly explored all the possibilities, are still unable to retrieve or generate a solution.

2. The second phase occurs suddenly and unexpectedly. After a break in mental fixation or re-evaluation of the problem, the answer is usually retrieved.

There are also two theories for how people arrive at the solution during a Eureka moment. The first is the Progress Monitoring Theory (PMT) where a person will analyse the distance from their current state to the goal state, and once they realise that they cannot solve the problem on their current path, they will seek alternative solutions. In complex issues this usually occurs late in the challenge. The second way is through the Representational Change Theory (RCT). Here, the problem solver has a low probability of a successful outcome, as they use inappropriate knowledge while establishing unnecessary constraints on the task/s. Only once relaxed on these limitations, can they bring real insight into working memory to solve a problem. The PMT theory being more suited to multiple step problems, and the RCT more suited to the single step problems.

Problem-solving requires insight (non-linear problems) and increased activity in the right cerebral hemisphere as compared with problem-solving that doesn't require insight (linear problems). In particular, increased activity was found in the right hemisphere anterior superior temporal gyrus. I've been interested in moments of Eureka for a while now because with the moment itself comes a real sense of achievement, euphoria and self-worth. We know that a quiet mind allows the weak connections of non-conscious processing to rise to awareness. Thus, the act of coming back fresh to a problem is valuable in itself. New research by neuroscientist David Creswell from Carnegie Mellon sheds some more light on this phenomenon.

Creswell designed an experiment where three groups of people were asked to approach the same problem in different ways – in this case, choosing the best vehicle for a given set of criteria. The first group had to make an instant decision. The second decided at leisure, after pondering the various options and finding what they considered to be the best fit. A third group was briefly distracted by a simultaneous, though not taxing, task. It was the third group who did best, despite their conscious thought processes being engaged on something else, due to the freedom this gave their unconscious to adopt novel approaches to the problem. This unconscious brain activity (unconscious neural reactivation) during the decision-making process was seen on fMRI scans of their brains. What this shows is that briefly stepping away from thinking about a problem can positively affect decision making and hence problem-solving.

So to the bit that I'm trying to drive us towards: *Designing complex flows, patterns, challenges, data capture and encouraged behaviours.* What we've been doing for decades now is this: we have tried to simplify complex tasks. This should be encouraged – we do wish to make complicated things simpler but what if we're missing the trick of building in other mechanisms for helping audiences solve complex challenges... like telling them to 'stop'? Some classic examples might be filling out application forms online, managing an investment portfolio, or writing a book like this one.

We have a lot of analytics running within our digital experiences, ones that track everything an audience does. From where they click, to how long they dwell... and we even know where they came from to arrive at the challenge, so we can then derive if they're slick or if they're thick. It's how we learn about their behaviour and make our systems smarter. So why wouldn't we turn that same machine learning back on the audience? We could, for example, tell them when they're in a bad spot. If we spot erratic or confused behaviour that implies someone is over-thinking or struggling to solve a problem, why not just prompt the person to take a break? Allowing people to continue pushing at a problem consciously when we should be allowing people to go off and ignore the problem is worth a moment's thought. If we do this, we also tend to realise that audiences get better outcomes – and faster, with less effort. This is the difference between power and force. Force tends to be about doing the most to get the most – but encourages exhaustion and a drain, compared with power, which is about alignment, and doing the least amount via positioning to generate the most significant benefit for the many. Designing more non-linear problems for people to solve, rather than making things too easy and instantaneous for people also encourages something called 'happiness'.

Being asked if they are happy can make people feel uncomfortable. It musters feelings of irritation and aggravation. I've even seen people become quite aggressive when being asked. It's one of those: *how much money do you make* questions, I think. How many people have you slept with? Perhaps because of happiness's said *importance* culturally, combined with it not tending to be something we spend a lot of time dissecting, it becomes a passing concern – especially with the speed of our modern world. The existentialists spent their lives studying it; the self-help industry has learnt how to make billions from it. If you wish to see more of it – then factor it into your design.

The science of happiness has undoubtedly received a considerable amount of attention in the last decade. Perhaps because it *is* that almost everyone would like to be happier. But where to begin? A lot of research that has emerged is showing how happiness can be measured objectively and over time, and that there is a strong correlation between happiness and the experience of *meaning* and that there are things we can do to increase our levels of joy and meaning.

Martin Seligman, Director of the Penn Positive Psychology Centre, suggests a simple equation might do it. H = S + C + V. Our enduring levels of happiness (H) are determined by our happiness set point (S), life circumstances (C) and intentional or voluntary activities (V). Sonja Lyubomirsky, researcher and author of The How of Happiness attached percentages to these components. She believes that a 'set point', || or happiness level determined by birth or genetics accounts for fifty percent of our potential happiness; with marital status and circumstances of earnings etc. defining just ten percent, and the remainder coming from intentional activities or things we can do to change our happiness levels. So it further backs up the need to design in non-linear interactions into everything we do. Help people grow, challenge them—change them.

⌘

We're building a lot of digital 'stuff' at the moment and there are a lot of factors that are often overlooked in the conception and creation of the things we build. I've talked at length about designing to overcome fears as well as the different types of problem-solving that help us evolve, but the third and possibly most important pillar of design is 'motivation'.

You know that sense of drive that energises our actions? Essential goals can take a frustrating amount of time and effort to achieve, and the mere thought of such exertion can be enough to put someone off a particular task. It's often believed that motivation is a state that is strictly psychological, and it is, but it's also biochemical: the opposing drives to act or not to act are being ultimately governed by the brain's perception of whether, on balance, the pros are higher than the cons of taking a given action.

Motivation is one of the most exciting behaviours for human-focused digital to consider and encourage. What inspires people to push forward? What invisible force keeps you accountable, despite boredom and roadblocks? To trace the source of motivation, let's begin in the brain where neurotransmitters spark chemical messages to keep us alert and on task. One specific neurotransmitter that plays a vital role in motivation is called dopamine. I've mentioned dopamine's role as a pleasure neurotransmitter. Its influence is felt in many areas, from memory and learning, to behaviour and mood but significant among these is motivation. It is the action of dopamine along the so-called mesolimbic pathway that causes the brain to flag up a critical decision point – where the individual recognises that they must act to ensure a good, rather than bad outcome in a given situation. Dopamine performs its task before we obtain rewards and not after we reach a goal, meaning that its real job is to encourage us to act and motivate us to achieve something good or avoid something terrible.

So it's scientifically proven that if we can design ways of encouraging an audience to persevere and push forward in small incremental directions, we can do mighty things but if our designed services stop short of pushing the audience over that threshold, then we may inadvertently have created the reverse effect.

'Rewards' have long been touted as a compelling incentive that drives people to dig deeper and return more. While this may make sense for repetitive tasks and linear problem solving, rewards don't quite resonate with non-linear problem solving when any rudimentary cognitive skill is needed to complete the task.

Being told you are performing well releases dopamine too – so designing that system of feedback, which continuously gives the audience a virtual thumbs up, is an essential thing. It's why I love the Push Notification feature on mobile phones – it's the most incredible way of letting someone know, periodically, that they're doing well at something. Use and abuse it. In marketing terms, it's the new CRM. Another good way of designing out functions that play to an audience's belief system is to recognise the different types of motivation that drive all the experiences we create. Most people will never feel very motivated to begin something but the way the brain works is that it will naturally start to produce dopamine as you start to get things done.

There are many proverbs along the lines of 'a journey of a thousand miles begins with a single step'. By acknowledging that dopamine ensures that each tiny step is rewarded and that we don't need to wait to achieve our goal to receive this reward, we can see that designing experiences that reward incremental steps towards the goal makes sense. People will be motivated to progress by these small rewards received along the way. Equally, we need to design each level to be achievable, and the first step is the most important to reward of all because it motivates you to continue.

By designing experiences that have a lot of small feedback loops, what we are doing is rewiring the brain to attach a dopamine response to all the little steps and not just the big ones. Getting your audience to be motivated and to persevere with a task is to understand what drives them in the first place. Start every new experience by asking them that very question and then acting on it. People's motivation can be anything from 'I want to be financially secure' to 'I want to send my son to the best school possible'. The secret to success is building trust by asking the questions that uncover the truth. This may seem easy enough, but the problem is we never actually ask that question. Furthermore, if someone does tell us their needs, we have an obligation to always think about how we can help them achieve those goals, which can only be fulfilled by an incredibly intelligent system.

Mastery should be acknowledged: when you can see progress in your effort, it further motivates you. Progress is the single most powerful motivator in meaningful work. Put simply, people want to see how far they've come, so we should ensure that they get this kind of feedback regularly and acknowledge the effort that has gone into the task so far. Conversely, motivation is severely affected by an apparent lack of progress, and the energy with which they initially engaged with the task will dwindle if they don't know how much longer it will take. By making this clear, even the most reluctant starter can be motivated to pursue the task through to its completion. These incremental feedback points give people a sense of control over the task – they're engaging with it because they want to.

In your design work, when you're asking audiences to set goals, make sure that you are considering and baking in the following rules to help hack motivation appropriately. All tasks and goals should be:

1. Realistic: goals should be based on their abilities and circumstances.

2. Possible: don't establish constraints that make the realistic unrealistic.

3. Flexible: help the audience anticipate bumps in the road and then help them to work around them.

4. Measurable: give them a target in mind, so they know when they have reached their goal.

5. Under your control: set goals based on their values, interests, and desires. Target things where they can control the outcome.

11. ALL TALK AND NO BUTTONS

'We seldom realise, for example, that our most private thoughts and emotions are not our own. For we think in terms of languages and images which we did not invent, but which were given to us by our society.' Alan W. Watts

We spent so much time focusing on creating glass barriers between people and their goal that we may have unintentionally missed the single most significant thing that separates us from other species. No matter the gender, race, or religion of a person—unlike other beings—we have a sense of curiosity: we try to understand the meaning of life, search for acceptance and gratification, and get to grips and accept the inevitability of our mortality. In doing so, we spend a lot of time—talking.

What if we could use digital design to help us all get back to having a good old-fashioned conversation, instead of all the 'browsing' and 'clicking' of stuff? People are pretty good at conversing. We use conversations to make or maintain relationships, to share or receive information, and to persuade each other to do things.

On the grand scale of things, we are evolutionary babies: all of 200,000 years old, for goodness sake! Modern civilisation as we know it is only about 6,000 years old, and even though we're getting good at all this 'technical stuff', the best thing we've ever learned to do right from the off was to talk. We evolved to do it with combinations of spoken words, written text, nonverbal sounds, physical gestures, and facial expressions—and we've had a lot of practice at it. So why don't we just digitise that instead? Amplify what we all do brilliantly, and stop creating lots of digitised product that we don't naturally understand?

Your health needs it too—there's enough research that shows people who talk more are often happier than those who don't. A good gossip every day releases endorphins that make you feel naturally more comfortable and happy.

This is predominantly why a 'conversational experience' is always going to be more effective. All this noise around Artificial Intelligence, Virtual Assistants and ChatBots isn't hype; it's just obvious. People were already ripe for it by being conversational creatures, to begin with. We *know* how to chat. We've been talking to our devices for years, but it wasn't until very recently that those interfaces also became able to *respond* with any credibility—we just hit the perfect intersection between technology and humanity. Dialogue-based interaction, either spoken or written, using your phone, tablet or computer (and very soon, the in-ear interface) is here and is not likely to go away. But of course with all these new ideas, the risk is that designers just dive on it because it's a *shiny thing* without truly understanding the psychology behind what makes a *good conversation*; and that's where we'll also see a lot of failures in this space. It's easy to forget that we're not digitising behaviour—we're behaving in a digital world. Is it not time, therefore, to return to basics and learn to talk again?

As simple as a conversation might seem, being human is a lot more complicated than it first appears and so conversational interfaces require designers and developers to leave behind current practices and adopt an entirely new mindset. I started the book by talking about looking outside your comfort zone. This is another excellent example of that. You need to look towards language, social psychology and linguistics for answers. The familiar design patterns we used when we were chopping up pictures and making them wobble around screens won't work in a conversation-driven interface. As the visual design is demoted in favour of words, what you say and how you say it will become more crucial than ever.

Recent success stories like Amazon's Alexa are excellent examples of conversational technology that amplifies the personality of the bot. Amazon spent a lot of time on the design of Alexa's character so people would feel comfortable with it, which we covered in the earlier chapter.

But, with the rise of messaging platforms like Facebook Messenger, Telegram, and Slack—bots that communicate with people by sending and receiving messages for all sorts of uses—it's going to be fascinating to watch how this space evolves. More often than not, designers are spending almost no time crafting the perfect personality—the bit that makes things like Alexa work well.

Chat interfaces powered by Natural Language Processing, Natural Language Understanding and Machine Learning are reaching the point of being 'OK' at holding down conversations with people, but there's no way they'll pass a Turing Test (to pass the Turing Test a machine has to be capable of lying, as well as telling the truth!), but they probably don't really need to be more than OK. In fact, the obvious flaws of an Ai may be precisely what make them work well (they just need to observe and react to what's being said to them, not lead or attempt to be smarter than they are). The time is ripe for conversational experiences, precisely because we can still identify Ai for what it is—we don't feel deceived. As Asimov predicted, '*We like robots that can be readily identified as robots*' and so the key to the conversational experience may be a transparently bot-like personality providing simple responses, rather than something so smart it's intimidating or uncomfortable.

Conversation is really a term that refers to the back and forth interaction through which two parties come to understand each other. That's the rub of what makes a conversation good—the back and the forth. So designing experiences that create that dialogue, although hugely complicated, is what you want to be striving for.

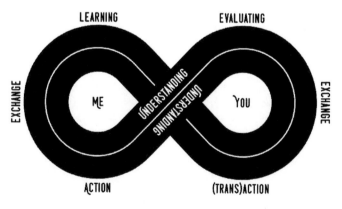

Adapted from an original piece by Paul Pangaro, 'Designing for Conversation', presented at Interaction 17, New York, February 2017

You don't need to be a social scientist to get a conversational experience right on the basics, just go back to what you already know, and you'll find your groove. Remember that a conversation goes nowhere unless you have a partner who listens to what you're saying and responds in a way that keeps the conversation going.

Building a relationship with someone is the key. Relationships are dynamic and multidimensional. Relationships develop over time as trust and insight increase. The most valuable relationships are ones in which people feel the most comfortable, most understood and the most empowered. Intelligent voice assistants or agents should be created with these relationship contexts in mind. It is important that we seek to establish a symbiotic relationship between an Ai powered agent and the end human. The words uttered by the machine need to form a relationship that shows respect, and understanding of the needs and context the people using them. We need to view this technology as a collaborator, a partner, a companion and not a rival or servant.

A good discussion is constructed by a speaker and a listener; each doing their part. It should be constructed with respectful, engaging, and enriching content. You learn something. You teach something. Your knowledge increases. Your curiosity is piqued. You relish the time spent together, and that is what you should be striving for – to design something that makes people feel like their time was invested well.

Let me give you the eight areas that I focus on when I design conversational experience. They might help you create some engaging conversations and get something more than a different type of interface shaped like bubbles into of your product.

Always *open* well

The opening gambit is also the key to all success. Get comfortable with Daniel Kahneman's 'Two-Question Technique'; always start by asking people about something positive in their life. Only after they reply should you ask them how they're feeling about life in general. A positive answer to the first question will lead to them feel more positive about their life in general when you ask the second question. Any emotionally significant question that alters a person's mood will have the same effect.

By being specific and leading the conversation in this way, you can also overcome the single most significant flaw of the conversational experience—natural language processing. Humans don't speak or write in perfect grammar that is free of typos. They use slang and nuance to express what they want—aspects that can make even the most powerful computer struggle. Machines just aren't good at engaging with all the quirks we've picked up over the last 200,000 years: accents, lousy grammar, and colloquial expressions. The main issue with natural language processing is that even if your Ai gets 80% of the sentences right, it will fail in the remaining 20% in a foolish, non-human way. Even if your error messages are witty and fun, people will still get frustrated. We're getting closer to having machines that can understand those oddities, but we're still quite far from it. Flip it—get the conversations perfect for the 20% of standard and regular queries and not the 80%.

Design your conversation to *give* information

This approach includes expressions of emotions and discussions of intent, as well as simple task-oriented requests—'Please give us more information so we can help you better.' Also, knowing when someone is giving you information is important because it leads to the question of what they want or expect you to do with the information. In the case of a customer telling you they are unhappy, they may be signalling that they want something to change—or they may just be venting and wanting to be heard. But if you don't factor in the reaction to your request for action—it's not a dialogue, it's just a prompt disguised as chat bubble.

Design your conversational experience to *get* information

Someone who says something to get information won't necessarily pose it in the form of a question. 'Tell me about…' is one way that a request for information can arrive in the form of a statement. The information being sought may be your opinion, your assessment, or your best guess. It's not always going to be hard and fast facts that someone wants. They may be gauging the to ascertain your willingness to act before they ask you to do something.

Get people to *do* something

It is imperative that the conversation you create is designed to get someone to do something. This is where we get into the guts of why people say things: to create actions on the part of other people. These steps are typically produced by giving information—but in those cases, the desired effects may not be readily apparent. The person asking may be counting on a specific response. Other times, the speaker's motivations are obvious: 'come here', as a parent might say to a child or 'kiss me, fool', as someone might say to a lover.

Make people *feel* good

If you don't design your conversations to make someone feel good, then don't bother with them at all. Compliments are the purest manifestation of this. It's just common human courtesy and all too often the experiences that are developed using the conversational paradigm leave out the essential courtesies that separate human interaction from the animalistic.

Get people to talk about *themselves*

You have to encourage people to talk about themselves—mainly because it can trigger the same sensation of pleasure in the brain as food or money. People do love to talk about themselves, once you tip them over the edge. In some of the experiments we've been conducting with conversational interfaces over the last 18 months, one of the things we've really started to observe in the data is that a lot of people are actually more comfortable speaking about themselves to a bot—even one that's a bit dumb—than face-to-face or using voice. It's because people don't have to be spontaneous in their replies and because they don't feel judged for the speaking skill-set they have. In a lot of cases, people also feel like they can communicate more efficiently using words on a screen or a voice in a box than in 'real' conversations.

We studied a group of volunteers using mental health chatbot we created called {SU}. We told half the volunteers it was controlled by a person—like a puppet. We told the other half it was fully computer-controlled—totally automated using Ai—and there was no human involved at all. The volunteers who thought they were talking just to the computer engaged in less 'impression management' and displayed emotions like frustration and sadness more freely and more opening. It turns out that people enjoy self-disclosure when it feels anonymous or safe.

Give *feedback* and ask more questions

If you use questions to guide people toward the errors in the thinking process and allow them to come up with the solution themselves, they're less likely to feel threatened and more likely to follow through. Don't assume to know all the answers—you won't, so ask for guidance and advice. New research shows that guidance seeking is a surprisingly effective strategy for exercising influence when we lack authority. In one of our experiments, when we focused the chat on the goal of getting a sale, only 8 percent of conversations reached a successful agreement. But when we asked the buyers for advice on how to meet their goals, 42 percent achieved a successful agreement. Asking for help encouraged greater cooperation and information sharing, turning a potentially contentious negotiation into a win-win deal. Seeking help is among the most effective ways to influence peers, superiors, and subordinates.

Be a good gossip

Don't forget to gossip (but positively). Research shows what we say about others colours how people see us. Compliment people and you're likely to be viewed favourably. Complain, and you're likely to be associated with those negative traits you complain about. When you make small talk and gossip, listeners unconsciously associate you with the characteristics you are describing, ultimately leading to those traits being 'transferred' to you. So bots should only say positive and pleasant things about the focused situation, and will consequently be seen as a kind person/bot. In contrast, any negativity, and people will unconsciously apply the negative traits and incompetence to the conversations (and ultimately you/your product). Bots have to make a negative sound positive.

Speech is a critical aspect of being human—*a whisper doesn't cut it.* Designing conversational experiences is hard because the concept of a conversation is by its nature straightforward and we pride ourselves in designing complex solutions to simple challenges. Building conversational interfaces don't just come with technological challenges—like Natural Language Processing—they also have lots of social ones. As the designers of these conversations, it's our responsibility to solve this part of the problem—to craft the perfect personality and dialogue flow.

It may be our actions that define us, but it is our reaction that changes the course of things. Study what makes a good conversation, not what technology platform is the biggest and brightest, and you'll start to find the sweet spot for making your idea resonate with the humans consuming it.

Remember this—you can't get away from the value of human expertise, wisdom, and our unique problem-solving ability; it's what caused us to evolve to where we are today. So start planning your conversational experiences by powering them with real humans, doing 100 percent of the work, on day one. Introduce natural-language-powered bots later to automate the 20 percent of the most frequent questions, or just to do the on-boarding part. Then later—much later—when you have accumulated a trove of dialogue data, you can move up the automation to take over more of the requests. *Embrace the Mechanical Turk.*

12. THE BEST THINGS IN LIFE ARE FREE

'Lock up your libraries if you like; but there is no gate, no lock, no bolt that you can set upon the freedom of my mind.' Virginia Woolf

Digital design, and the various disciplines within, has been driven by a desire to control the actions of the people 'using' the service. We create tunnels and funnels and shovel people into the fat end of the machine and guide them through a journey and a process to achieve what we want (or think we want) them to achieve. In a lot of cases, this is a necessary thing to do. For example, sometimes it's important that people are guided through an important task, like paying a bill or filling in a complex application process without distractions. Designing something paternalistic in these cases is a good thing to do.

I believe that the design of digital services will always affect the lives and wellbeing of the people consuming them and of society at large, whether implicitly or explicitly. This is true in a trivial sense, since products are meant to fulfil existing and conscious needs. But it is also true in a less obvious way, since products engrained in our lives also affect us due to the way they influence our behaviour, attitudes and needs. By designing things that guide people along journeys, one of the changes we make is the erosion of people's 'freedom'. Not freedom in the libertarian sense, but in the sense of our ability to choose. Recent studies show that personal independence and freedom are more important for a person's welfare, in a lot of cases, than considerations of wealth or health. So designers really need to be mindful and try hard not to erode the freedoms of choice by designing in the paternalistic sense as a default, perhaps leading to dissatisfaction and frustration.

Design can be used to influence and improve wellbeing, but going too far over that line leads us to the ethical arguments found between determination and freedom. I'm determined to achieve my goal, but I want the freedom to find my own path. Allowing people free will to make choices without any prior prejudice, inclination, or disposition is so important to what makes us human. Our choices are not only ultimately determined by designers but also morally determined by our own nature. Designers are just the people creating the opportunities to explore one's own freedoms.

However, when designs encourage an explicit and intended interference with how people live their lives, this also raises ethical questions. How desirable is it that designers can intervene in a person's behaviour? Should the designer's influence on people's behaviour be avoided at all times, or should we rather see it as a core responsibility of designers to encourage the behaviour that we want to see?

Most of us cannot yet fully comprehend the importance of the fact that we are free to behave as we choose and free to express ourselves in a manner that society deems acceptable. We're free to decide and control aspects that concern us directly. It is said that those who do not understand the value of their freedom are actually prisoners of their own ignorance and inability to act independently according to their own will. Helping people to value their freedom should start with the services we design on their behalf. Let's start making people aware of their freedom to be themselves, by using all this amazing digital design we're spewing into the world as the vehicle for that message: by making the interactions less cluttered with constraint and more fluid by nature.

Throughout my career as a designer, I've often defaulted to the parental way of designing interfaces. I chose the destiny for a whole audience. I used the ill-fated 'persona' to determine how I wanted huge, homogenous swathes of people to behave. We often find that we do this to the detriment of something that makes us tick and thrive—we love our freedom. When you create a funnel, you're already eating into people's psyche. How often have you stopped to think about that? What about the fact that, as humans, we want the freedom to explore: the freedom to fail? We want the freedom to make our own choices and decisions—because that's what makes us human. Think about the great semantic diversity of the term freedom and the complexity of our social life and the multiple relationships we have with other people. Let our digital world be full of the same ideals. Being given freedom is important because it also gives everyone the opportunity to participate in decisions of interest. I get really frustrated by things like investing platforms that, by design and regulation, only play to the elite few who understand the language and the jargon. Where are the opportunities to invest for people who don't process the jargon or know what investing is? Because I don't understand it, you won't give me the opportunity to engage with it and that's more than just bad design, it's an infringement of my fundamental human right to achieve all that I could achieve. It needs to stop. It needs to be approachable for all. To level us all out and give us all the opportunities to thrive—to give us all freedom to be the best we can be. Even a lot of apps and services for everyday things like games or way-finding take away the freedom to engage on my own terms and in my own way, because they've instinctively been designed to appeal to a certain audience. They don't encourage freedom because by their nature, they've been designed by people from that background who only know what they know.

There are positive examples too—social media by design is a relatively basic interaction. You get given the platform and you choose how to use it to engage with your chosen audience. That's good. It has wide appeal and broad strokes. I also know a lot of designers who care deeply about the effects of their designs and the wellbeing of the audience and they design with that in their minds.

We are free spirits, therefore it is in our nature to seek to be completely free, at least at some point in time. Freedom gives us happiness because the state of being free is aligned with our true nature as human beings. So stop designing restraints and start designing opportunities to allow a person to flourish. Freedom is also subjective: we are only able to value it, in as far as we can acknowledge how much it's worth to us. One of my fears for the current generations, being born into the digital world that we have created and manipulated, is that we spent a lot of time creating those funnels and therefore I ask myself whether we have allowed generations to grow up feeling constrained by what we decided was right and wrong for them.

I talk about happiness by design a lot. What I mean by that is that we should always be designing in a way that is mindful of a person's feelings as they use the products we create. 'How do you want someone to feel?' not 'How do you want someone to behave?'. There are many things that are sources of happiness, and freedom is one of them. Just having access to information via the Internet is a brilliant source of happiness for a lot of people and we should celebrate the infrastructures we created to give us so much opportunity. One piece of analysis done by British researchers from the U.K.'s Chartered Institute for Technology even suggested that technology has an enabling and empowering role in people's lives, demonstrated in the way it increases their sense of freedom and control, which in turn has a positive impact on well-being or happiness. It's ironic then that once you enter that plane of freedom called the Internet, and start engaging with something designed by other people, you are often faced with walls of asymmetrical paternalism. Asymmetric paternalism is a concept used to evaluate when a behavioural intervention should be made. A rule or regulation is asymmetrically paternalistic if it creates large benefits for those who make errors, while imposing little or no harm on those who are fully rational. By its nature, it creates a constraint of which we are all a part and willingly accept. A fascinating dichotomy.

Learning by experience is fun and its good for our health. Therefore we need to allow people to explore and also to fail. Help them fail: to make mistakes and learn from them. But more than that, experience and failure is a vital part of our development as individuals. Freedom of thought, opinion, creativity and faith are fundamental human rights, which are found in the constitutions of numerous acts of international significance. So are we not, as digital designers, eroding freedom when we create experiences that are linear by nature and try to prevent failures? We set out to create maps and paths that are funnels through systems that are predefined, in order to get someone from A to Z.

From our earliest years we learn by exploring, experimenting, trial and error – a process that brings us joy when we succeed and causes us to remember the pathways that led to a successful outcome more readily than if those paths are presented to us as the 'correct' way to do something. The curriculum for early years teaching focuses on 'awe and wonder'; allowing children to examine their environment and marvel at what they can achieve within it. In some senses, designers are like these children and it can be seen that those approaching the latest technologies with a sense of joyful exploration – and encouraging people to use it in the same way – are succeeding because they are instinctively offering the most satisfying and memorable path. People thus feel empowered and in control of both their approach to the technology and the social aspect of the experience. In allowing people to find their own solutions, designers provide a shared experience of freedom that unites young and old, rich and poor, the educated and less educated in society – truly enfranchising users, without the constraints that they are accustomed to face in their day-to-day experience of technology.

We've come a long way since the assumption that technology, and in particular the internet, is the playground of the young, and the received wisdom that technology has nothing to offer the older user in terms of enjoyment, engagement and social satisfaction. Increasingly, the social aspect of the digital world is proving a draw for people of all ages, happy to explore, befriend and play – much as curious children do when making discoveries about the world that surrounds them. And there's a whole, vast digital universe out there for us to explore; making our own connections, free to seek out our own digital pathways and take control of the way we use technology in new ways. We should be designing to take advantage of this instinctive willingness to learn through the use of everyday language, rather than jargon; through encouragement and reassurance, rather than error messages and indications of failure. We should be examining our designs to see whether they encourage our users to adopt a joyful, childlike approach of exploration and discovery.

When you get to designing those screens and flows and experiences that you now want to encourage someone to feel free in, remember that freedom also comes in many forms. For example, economic freedom refers to the opportunity for people to act freely in their double act as producers and consumers. Personal freedom refers to the right of any person to refuse the interference of others (as individuals or representatives of an authority) in their private life or during certain private activities. How often do we give people the option at the start of an experience either to self-direct or be directed? Wouldn't that be an amazing 'norm' to offer everyone, no matter how experienced or not they are? Maybe Ai experiences are the future of freedom, because they allow a new, more targeted and tailored way of creating fluid experiences, rather than fixed ones.

Once you get take the approach of designing for an experience that offers people more freedom, if you truly believe in that freedom, you must learn to adopt a relaxed mindset—both as the designer and also from the perspective of the business sanctioning the output. You will be challenged and attacked on many occasions but because this is the reality, we must accept it and at the same time enjoy it. We must reject what we do not like and move on, without self-imposed limits on what we are thinking. If we do not agree to a subject, it does not mean that there is no value in it. This is the essence of a more human approach to design. If we want to create a new value system for design, then we must be willing to give up what we already have. It is impossible to win without taking any risks. So creating design that is untethered and riddled with twists and turns is a gamble but also a huge opportunity for designers and businesses to free themselves of the worry of failure. Accept it's going to fail and people will find a way through, using their best wit and judgement. How liberating for all?

An emerging trend towards *'Persuasive'* design

For me though, designing with constraints is not the riskiest or most worrying aspect of the freedom and achievements of the both designer and consumer. The greatest risk is this skew towards some new, dark approaches to 'user-influencing design'.

'Ipsa scientia potestas est': if, as Francis Bacon said, knowledge itself is power, then the knowledge of how to forge a path through the wonders of modern technology is an opportunity that should be available to everyone. Digital designers can make this happen: it is not only a possibility; it is essential to help businesses to convey their messages to a diverse population. Technology can thus be used in a persuasive manner but with the lightest of touches, engaging people because they are willing to engage and 'nudging' them towards desirable choices in an ethical and holistic manner. There is no need to direct and force the path that the user will take: instead it is preferable that they arrive at the desired outcome as a result of their own choices. Designers should be helping businesses to decide whether the guidance they build into their systems is optimising desired behaviour or forcing the user down a pre-ordained route. The question should always be, 'Is this approach ethical and persuasive or has the balance of power tipped away from the user? Will people feel they have enjoyed the experience and arrived at the conclusion of their choice or have we coerced them into choosing what we wanted them to choose?'

Technology, happiness and our freedom are in an intimate relationship. Design and technology can give direction to a way of living and can enhance our freedom. But freedom is also a fundamental aspect of happiness that seems in conflict with the dominating aspects of some technology. The challenge is to understand how to design influencing technology that does not negate freedom. We need to design technology that mediates our lives by giving specific content to freedom. Designing for freedom, then, should attempt not only to influence human actions and decisions in desirable directions, but also to make it possible for people to develop an active and critical relationship with these influences. Rather than designing possibilities to opt out, it is important to think about multiple ways to opt in. And beyond creating transparency about designer intentions, and the methods and effects of persuasion, it is important to enable people to develop a critical relationship with these intentions, methods, and effects.

Taking this all on board, an approach to *human focused digital* is basically the concept that, metaphysically and morally, we are all autonomous beings, people who operate independently, not controlled by others or by outside forces. That should be embraced and encouraged, not whittled down and eroded.

13. TAOISM 2018

'Nature loves courage. You make the commitment and nature will respond to that commitment by removing impossible obstacles. Dream the impossible dream and the world will not grind you under, it will lift you up. This is the trick. This is what all these teachers and philosophers who really counted, who really touched the alchemical gold, this is what they understood. This is how magic is done, by hurling yourself into the abyss and discovering it's a feather bed.' Terence McKenna

Have you ever started a financial plan? If you're anything like I was, we've all started financial plans, 'started' being the operative word. It goes like this: you've set out with the best intentions but failed to keep the momentum going. That's basically it. You've stagnated, wallowed and then… started up again. Relying on motivation and willpower doesn't work and I know that's not something to preach – I'm coming up against a self-help industry that banks billions, but I'm not selling an ideology, I'm facing the reality of the situation, and it wasn't always a habit of mine. The denial mechanisms we place it in can in fact be quite sophisticated, and the positions we learn to defend – well argued. It becomes convenient to explain to ourselves and others our current position, financially. The reality, though, is not so convenient. When you begin any new self-improvement program, your enthusiasm is high and you're motivated by the pleasure of what you want or the pain of what you don't want. But motivation naturally diminishes with time, like the creatine housed in your muscular biology to take you through the first thirty minutes of your gym workout, you eventually, inevitably run out of gas.

Something like financial planning needs to become a habit like brushing your teeth, and not a fad like dieting or Zumba. Once a habit is established, people find themselves doing it effortlessly. Remember, the four stages of learning:

1. Unconsciously-incapable
2. Consciously-incapable
3. Consciously-capable
4. Unconsciously-capable

A lot of the time when we are at '1', we think we are at '4' but '1' eventually ends and rather than recognise that we were only ever at '1', we go onto other things and become '1s' at those. Instead, see yourself through the four stages and become 4s at as many of them as you can.

Setting big goals is exciting but starting with small, boring goals is more likely to lead to success and that long-term goal of being able to do something so naturally, that you haven't got to think becomes as natural to you as… well, whatever that thing is that you are a 4 at. Bench pressing? Roller skating? Pencil drawing? Think of that thing that you can do with ease, and realise that all you have to do is see yourself through the stages and you will finish there and once you are a 4, you are always a 4. Yes, it is like learning to ride a bike. Does anyone need to teach you again how to brush your teeth? Taking small actions tricks your brain, and this is the key. Your subconscious likes to be in control and because of this, it doesn't like change. Remember, your subconscious is like your parents: it likes to be in control, and it doesn't like change – unless it is in accord with what is 'right' and 'healthy'. Learning to trust the subconscious and allowing it to guide us forward is the healthiest way to zip-line, instead of the more fast food, big changes that we are too often encouraged to run within a world addicted to sugar, coffee, and anything fast – especially if it's faster than the other person's fast. A big change sets up subconscious resistance, but you can sneak a small change by it, and there is an art to this. If you ask neuroscientists or researchers, they will likely tell you that change rarely happens overnight by changing something in its entirety. The best path to sustainable behavioural change is taking small steps, moving slowly and realising that all things are marathons – not sprints.

Now we have a far greater understanding of the human brain that we design services with micro changes and more importantly introduce micro-actions – actions so small and simple anyone can do them.

Knowing how difficult it is to generate the willpower needed to 'get there', we as designers now have the power to not only nurture and initiate the willpower, but to lead a person through the endurance marathon, helping them retain engine fuel and getting them there injury free, risk free, again and again.

Your actions, you see, are a reflection of how your brain is wired to function. By changing an audience's actions – even if we start with a *micro*-action – you can actually start to reprogram the brain, and trigger a virtuous circle of more action. Changing subsequent actions thus becomes both easier and more likely to succeed. Some people don't like the idea of re-programming, and think of it as un-doing something but we can think of it along the lines of helping a person return to their natural constitution or original blueprint, one where they are cleaner and free to go at things in a way that has been unspoilt or undamaged by a trillion environmental attacks.

As designers, we're in the business of behavioural change and we want to try and create experiences that make the audience do only one daily action, but this can be thought of as being behavioural 'return' back to a person's natural order where they are completely capable and able to do anything. They'll soon start to notice that they become more conscious of other small things they could do better, so design for the mindset of 'what small thing could I do better today?'.

Not long ago it was thought that the brain stops learning after a certain age. Not true, proved Leonardo. Your brain in fact keeps learning throughout your entire life through a process called neuroplasticity – also referred to as brain plasticity, meaning the brain's ability to change at any age – for better or worse. As you would imagine, this flexibility plays an incredibly important role in our brain development (or decline) and in shaping our distinct personalities. Neuroplasticity happens when the brain's building blocks (neurons) connect with each other and keep the brain active.

Tony Buzan, author of *Master Your Memory* and *The Speed Reading Book* described da Vinci as a 'giant baby', because he always felt he could 'never stop learning more' and in the same way a baby would engage its full breadth of cortical skills available to it and not work within the confines of one field, so too can grown adults. Da Vinci was the great example of this. Due to the way we can box ourselves in with respect to a specific field of research, even the most academically advanced minds still hit cul-de-sacs with their work as their information can become in itself compartmentalised according to their field and the way they have been cultured to read into a thing. This produces a phenomenon where a smart intelligent academic with a high IQ can also be off with their findings. It seems that nobody is free from the need to constantly revise both how to see things, and how to go about things. Habits then are absolutely significant.

Designing for micro-actions is important because we do experience these hundreds of thousands of stimuli daily, and it is impossible for the brain to keep up. Focusing on small changes allows your brain to effectively start the process of neuroplasticity. Slowly... slowly...

⌘

Create, focus and complete—because your brain is really smart (and lazy). It is constantly trying to save effort by creating habits, so it's key to build the habits in that you do want, right? But why is the brain trying so hard to create habits? Because habits are 'pre-programmed' and require less energy. Energy conservation is a natural law and as mentioned the thing that separates power and force. Force is about doing the most to generate the most using the most – but doesn't always generate the most. Power is about doing the least to create the most and retaining the most energy while doing a thing. Another way of thinking about this is: do what is easiest, and not in a passive way, on the contrary: it requires tremendous focus to do very little. Have you ever tried to meditate? To help create habits, your task is to pick activities that are easy (which a micro-action is), then focus and repeat. Your actions re-program your brain. When you take action and succeed you get a sense of accomplishment, advancement, and other positive feelings. Your brain starts learning, and it makes you more ready and likely to take the next action, and thus triggers a virtuous circle of even more action.

As we age, our brains work less well, degeneration sets in and occasional forgetfulness can lead to anxiety and perhaps the onset of age-related conditions such as Alzheimer's. We might be just as curious and keen to learn as we were as young people but the brain can let us down as an organ. Meanwhile, the ability to learn is still present and many advocate the forming of beneficial habits to improve memory and retention of new information. How many people do you know who advocate crosswords or Sudoku to keep their little grey cells in tip-top condition? The brain's neuroplasticity is maintained and memory and cognition are improved by repetitive activities, especially those involving our senses. There are other things too; you know how a familiar scent can transport you back to childhood? That's the kind of sensory cue that we can use to our advantage. Mineral deficiencies can also contribute to degenerative conditions. The brain is housed in an insulating material known as myelin. Myelin is one hundred percent fat and is made of cholesterol, so feeding the brain the key omega fats are essential in helping the organ retain its necessary health. To endure all of the testing you are making it go through, make sure you keep some oil in the car – we don't want to exhaust our cars, we want to look after them, right? The avocado, coconut and fish are all loaded with the right fats and oils, as well as eggs, black seed oil and nuts. Feed the organ like any other!

Visual cues to remember are useful at any age. They need not be related to the activity you need to remember – perhaps you'll tie a knot in a piece of string to remind you to put the rubbish out for collection – but writing a note or leaving a Post-it on the TV to remind you to record a programme provides a visual cue for recalling that activity. By habitually carrying out these behaviours in reaction to a given trigger, we build neural pathways that allow us to follow the routine subconsciously. Once a habit is formed we do it routinely, without much thought. Can you see how we are transcending through the stages of learning?

The importance of visual cues as a trigger to perform an action or a routine is a form of problem-solving that can be incorporated into an approach to design. As a form of Taoism, designing for the journey – the 'way' – is critical to success. By considering the human experience along the way, we help to get them to where we want them to be. My slightly Darwinian take on the Tao is that humans follow a journey underpinned by three basic evolutionary needs or 'master motives.'

1. The need to get ahead and learn. Some individuals are more willing and able to be in charge of this destiny.

2. The need to get along and socialise, which promotes cooperation and makes us group-living animals. (Freud noted that although humans are social animals, living with others does not come easy. He compared people to a group of hedgehogs during the winter):

"They need to get close to each other to cope with the cold, but if they get too close, they end up stinging each other with their prickly spines."

This very rule is often the trickiest function to build. Audiences don't want to go it alone, but working with others does require some discomfort. Some tensions may arise by the desire of a person to be accepted and loved by other people.

3. Finally, humans like to have fun, which can also provide individuals with a formal system for finding meaning.

These three basic principles act as an ecosystem of knowledge, which works as a lens through which we see the world. Think about the little actions you design, how often and how few they are, but also how you categorise them. Somewhere between the size, the frequency and the type of actions (across the above three categories) is the answer to behavioural change—a journey of a thousand miles does begin with a single step. The key is to step. Tiptoe if you must—but keep it to a step.

DESIGN PRINCIPLES		EXPERIENCE PRINCIPLES
WHAT DO WE WANT USERS TO DO?	········▶	HOW DO YOU WANT PEOPLE TO FEEL?
MINIMUM VIABLE PRODUCT	········▶	MINIMUM VIABLE PERSONALITY
OPTIMISED JOURNEYS	········▶	ALL TALK & NO BUTTONS
CONTENT DRIVEN	········▶	QUESTION DRIVEN
SIMPLIFIED FORM AND FUNCTION	········▶	NO FORM AND FUNCTION
HCI (HUMAN COMPUTER INTERACTION)	········▶	HCR (HUMAN COMPUTER RELATIONSHIPS)
DO THINGS BETTER?	········▶	DO BETTER THINGS?

14. IF SOCRATES HAD SIRI... A FUTURE?

'Only you can control your future.' Dr Seuss

Emerging technology is enhancing and accelerating the process of communication as we enter a new phase, a new era in the on-going exploration of vast unknown territories of all experience, digital included. I'm not, you see, obsessed about digital. I'm into humanity, into exploring, into discovery and the stars and understanding the secrets—knowing more, ascending and the journey. Technology is just a tool, an extension of us that our genius has built. In no different a way than a pair of eyeglasses enhances sight, or a mosquito net defends like an anti-virus protection software programme, or a table makes it easier to eat food, or a mug to drink coffee, technology built by us for us is something we bring into manifestation through our genius to aid, service, de-stress, and enhance experience. It is the vehicle for us to access more and as we continue to make Artificial Intelligence a more contemporary subject and begin injecting it into everyday lives more, it will continually alleviate struggle until it begins to replace old with new and free us. Freedom, that's what I'm into – not servitude to devices that are *trying* to free me but are at fault in their design.

What is the missing glue that gives Ai the cadence to become accepted as an ambient part of our lives? I don't know for sure, but the emerging idea of 'emotional analytics' could be the answer to this missing link. Imagine an analytical construct living inside all of your devices that open up the next dimension of person-machine interaction – such as Moodies, for example – an app that analyses speech into compartments of mood, and since it focuses in on emotional state and not content, it is able to analyse more than just content. This ability to understand mood, attitude and emotional personality is disruptive in almost any category imaginable. People seem to intuitively know how to determine the mood of most people they interact with, but our machines don't. They do not know how we feel; they have no idea as to what we 'mean', and they are clueless when faced with deciphering whether a quickly uttered 'have a nice day' is in fact genuine. This emotional blind spot is not due to a lack of trying. Researchers and computer scientists have been struggling for decades to endow machines with these qualities that we as humans take for granted.

When we meet someone new, we use visual, verbal and other sensory cues to interpret mood and emotions. It is the dream of many a developer to be the first whose technology can accomplish this, and over the years some advances have been made toward this goal, such as text-to-speech. These days, the kind of technology in use in mobile phones and call centres can interpret the words in your questions and respond accordingly – but without reference to your emotional state. The transaction is factual, and it is interpreting your needs by means of a kind of look-up process: matching your words against its internal dictionary and then analysing your vocabulary and the semantics of what you've said. What's missing is the ability that humans have to use nuances in speech, gesture and expression to distinguish whether you're angry, sad or excited. So far, the first steps in sentiment analysis have relied on verbal cues alone. As far as physical cues are concerned, technology can match physical attributes like face shape and eye colour to distinguish one person from another but is limiting in its availability to discern the facial expressions that convey emotion and other messages to the human observer, such as a smile or a frown. The development of video messaging means that the physical expression of our emotions is available for interpretation. This is a big step forward for human understanding – how often have we failed to gauge the tone of written correspondence and responded inappropriately in the past? For these reasons, mixed with the work explored in different areas of psychology, psychologists will now play a significant role in programming, as the ways things are understood will themselves need to be programmed. Different things can be said in different ways with different agendas, and all of this space for interpretation, intention and objective makes sure that philosophy, psychology and the study of culture must be brought through and the Plato cave of the graphic designer needs to be in flux. The current challenge is finding ways for technology to interpret these same physical cues to the complex emotions we experience when communicating with others: a challenge that humans manage efficiently from birth.

In this near future, the pace of technological change will be so fast and far-reaching that human experience in this reality will be irreversibly altered. In Plato's Allegory of the Cave, the freed prisoner wants to help his enslaved friends who still live in the confines of the cave reality but lifting a person out of their cave and into the higher *real* has always required strategy and patience as well as an understanding of who we are, our emotional repressions and our psychological jails. As Ray Kurzweil writes, 'We will combine our brain power—the knowledge, skills, and personality quirks that make us human—with our computer power to think, reason, communicate, and create in ways we can scarcely even contemplate today.'

People will as if unconsciously, begin to free themselves of their interface screens and gravitate like iron filings being pulled by the invisible mother magnet – into the future where Ai lives: it is just out of manifestation, for now. Today, the relationship between a person and an interface is still a semantic one, characterised by meaning and expression rather than physical force. For the magic of the digital revolution to indeed take place, the computer needs to start representing itself to people in a language that they can truly understand. Pioneer of information technology, philosophy, and sociology Ted Nelson said it:

'Digital computers are literary machines; they work with signs and symbols, although this language, in its most elemental form, is almost impossible to understand. A computer thinks—if thinking is the right word for it—in tiny pulses of electricity, a zero or a one. Humans think in words, concepts, images, sounds, associations. A computer that does nothing but manipulate sequences of zeros and ones is nothing but an exceptionally inefficient adding machine.'

For the new relationship between us and technology to succeed, the trust will need to breathe through. We know technology can be relied on to follow instructions that we give it when we programme those in, but are we able to let go and trust the way technology arrives at a decision based on how it's been programmed and the languages innate to it, compared with our biased interjections to steer the ship? This seismic shift required for us to relinquish control and watch technology reach into the future makes us fearful. Perhaps this is the thing we need to address collectively, and not the potential for technology to wipe us out in an Ai hurricane. The emergence of healthy tech will thus grow in parallel with the emergence of healthy people. It is then not difficult to realise why and what technology currently is—a creation that *we* have built. It's then for us to change the content that is being projected onto the screen – if we are not enjoying the movie. It is not, you see, technology that is failing when we build killing machines, but the person who made or is using it at that moment. Technology is neither good nor bad; it is inanimate. Attaching judgement to material builds is, therefore missing the entire point and discussions concerning technology's position in aiding our evolution. Are we exploring into the future? And can we use tech to support this journey for the benefit of all the world's people, and indeed for the earth itself? These are the questions.

The logical development of the interface between humans and technology involves the ability to process language and emotion. This will inevitably mean the disappearance of the ubiquitous screen and a shift toward conversation. This kind of voice operating system is already with us, in the form of Siri on Apple devices. Developments in the near future will mean that Siri's children will thus be able to supply the answer we need when we ask a question: not just the many thousands of hits that search engines currently deliver, and from which we still have to select our ideal solution.

⌘

The development of Artificial Intelligence has been stop-start, from early predictions in the 1950s that we would be able to rely on technology to replace us in the workplace within decades, to the Ai winter when progress stalled due to lack of investment. Artificial Intelligence: it always has had the potential to reorganise our experience, here – in this reality and for some people, more than anything else; religions, political system—anything. Over the last twenty years, it has started to emerge as something that might change not only technology but also human behaviour—beyond recognition. I genuinely believe it's the key to unlocking the full potential of human-focused digital, so it is essential that we understand what Artificial Intelligence is, in order to understand what it is going to mean for design. Because now that it is here, we have a solid foundation to start creating more intelligent, invisible experiences that will make us more *human by design*. We are at the precipice of one of the most significant discoveries of development since we learnt how to light a fire.

The kind of Artificial Intelligence that is programmed to complete one task correctly is called Artificial Narrow Intelligence, and that concept is already with us – the oft-quoted example being Deep Blue, the computer that beats humans at chess but can't do anything else. The next step is to develop Artificial Intelligence to the stage where it can match a person's intellectual capacity across the whole range of tasks that we accomplish in everyday life, such as problem-solving, handling abstract concepts and learning from experience. Despite substantial investment, no computer has yet achieved this level, known as Artificial General Intelligence. The ultimate goal though – ASI, Artificial Super Intelligence or the ability to fuse levels of intellect that exceed our human capabilities with social skills and additionally, the judgement that allows it to deploy such intelligence wisely. Perhaps it will be that ultimately our AGI computers will teach themselves how to build ASI computers and then the whole universe begins to change – that's the potential we hold: that an eco-system of tech starts to grow out of itself, hence the fear of the 'bye bye humans' thing. Oxford philosopher and a current leading Ai thinker Nick Bostrom defines superintelligence as:

'An intellect that is much smarter than the best human brains in practically every field, including scientific creativity, general wisdom and social skills. Artificial Superintelligence ranges from a computer that's just a little smarter than a human to one that's trillions of times smarter—across the board. ASI is the reason the topic of Ai is such a hot potato topic and why the words immortality and extinction are often thrown in with the same breath in the discussion.'

Communication between people needs to be immediate, global, and expressive. Like a stream of water that finds a crack in the rock and flows through it, information will always find a way to develop a more efficient channel. Our digital conversations have almost imperceptibly morphed into a vibrant, evocative form of communication and when added into some of our existing communication channels, Artificial Intelligence is then going to adapt, until it becomes more like the communication we all globally need.

Artificial intelligence should not only underpin design thinking—but also enable the personality of the product or brand we need to create, to make digital products believable and approachable.

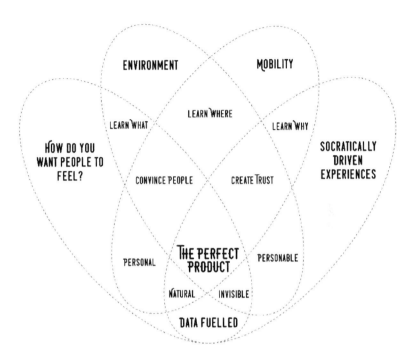

Coming at design and digital product development *just* from the perspective of the interface will no longer work. We have to factor in the elements that make digital truly—intelligent. We have to wrap a lot more concepts into our designs and think *Intelligently Artificial.*

15. THE CAVE

'Man – a being in search of meaning.' Plato

Behaviour is the range of actions and mannerisms made by people in conjunction with themselves or their environment, which includes the other people around as well as the (inanimate) physical environment. It is the response of a person to various stimuli or inputs, whether internal or external, conscious or unconscious, overt or covert, and voluntary or involuntary. From a human-focused perspective, behaviour consists of four essential elements: a person, operations (actions, activities) and interactions (relationships), and their properties. A behaviour can be represented as a behaviour vector, as all behaviours of a person or group of people can be represented as behaviour sequences and a multi-dimensional behaviour matrix.

From clocking our steps each day, to online shopping and finding recipes for cupcakes, we all use apps. Certain apps are able to track our behaviour and then predict purchasing habits and then prioritise things for us, such as results. As it stands, this is currently quite hit or miss. Anticipating requirements based on preferences that have previously been mined and understood based on who you are and what you want, and although the cost of development here is considerable, it could be that soon we'll be buying phones with apps that employ this kind of behavioural analytics to deliver an experience that is personalised, via the tech that we've built to actually understand a person (as opposed solely to what an ad campaign is pushing). Behaviours will be stored and shared across platforms, until eventually the experience of living in a city becomes as breezy as walking along a beach, free we will be again to walk as we won't be caught in the web of work we need to do moment to moment while it drowns us. Apps that communicate between one another, coupled with a lack of actual interfaces to process the data, seems to rule out the Cloud-based manipulation of the data. Instead, it is more likely that operating systems themselves will extract the information and behavioural data and then store it in what has come to be known now as The Cloud, and there it will be kept while being available too, as a profile of the person. That means this: if a person adds a new fitness app, it will have access to their profile to update preferences and trends and personalise the product experience in a way that is entirely immediate.

As anyone with an Apple Watch will tell you, though, it's all about the notifications, not the apps. The taps on my wrist make it abundantly clear just how dumb most notifications are. Fiona Spruill, VP Product, Meetup

Where most notifications use our location, our schedules, and our reading habits, to themselves upgrade, the 'now' type mentality spreads but once behavioural analytics and machine learning marry human-focused principles, the *now* mentality will leave and a world where notifications make us better people has space to develop.

What was the last new app you installed where you appreciated the notifications enough to keep them on? Mike Davidson, VP Design, Twitter

The next step in the evolution of conversational interfaces, powered by Ai and triggered by emotions in your data will be embedding functionality into conversations, allowing people to call a taxi or order flowers right from inside the messaging interfaces. Tasks like this would have traditionally fallen to apps, most of which were shoved into some dusty folder in the corner of your phone for that one time a year you needed to launch it.

The use of such apps is labour-intensive as things stand. Sending flowers, for example, must run through a process that demands things from us, and by the time we have downloaded the app and selected and placed the order, we then deal with the next obstacle because they are in fact now sold out, or the shop is closed. The next generation of interfaces, such as Siri and Google Now, will replace this untidy vehicle with a smoother ride as spontaneous interfaces using Ai emerge, drawing on people's profiles that have been built and analysed in preparation for even the most difficult of nightmare tasks. Imagine, for example, the work that can be lifted from our shoulders when buying a house, trying to move abroad or in time, the most efficient way to manage an entire business. The worry that we then won't have anything to do because everything is being handled for us is misleading. Technology can free us to realise who we are, and what we want to do. Facing this is the route of the concern because dealing with the reality of our own dharma, our life missions, is too terrifying for us, since then we would have to make that film, write that book, learn the piano or open that restaurant – but in an attempt to bury our callings, we repress technology's potential to free us.

When designing for this kind of smart experience, we have to consider really carefully the way someone interacts and controls the Ai. Keeping human-focused design principles in mind, the ideal experience needs to allow people to act naturally, using language and intonation they would normally use. Don't make people speak like a computer (as we've covered in previous chapters).

Many interactions with this new emerging smart technology will of course be task-oriented, but how people make requests will vary. This is an opportunity for Ai to connect the dots, and be aware of what the person will need and surface that information, rather than putting the person in the position of having to operate like a computer and lead the Ai to each dot. For example, if a person is initiating a task related to an appointment, do not make them ask to see her/his calendar. An Ai that has already learned the patterns and behaviours, can take the initiative in surfacing the calendar for the person in anticipation of their needs.

⌘

As we've previously covered, if your product does have a voice, and it was talking to your customers twenty-four hours a day, what voice would you want it to have? One that is polite? Strict? Funny? Would you want it to come off as paranoid or trusting? Modest or likeable? View your product as a *person* but unlike friends and family – here we get to choose what voice he/she has. The personality you build in turn guides the copywriting, the interface, and the feature set. Whenever you make a change, ask yourself if that change fits your app's personality. As we move away from screens, the personality of your product will have to become more automatic, anticipatory, and predictive.

But new and exciting opportunities also start to emerge when you consider that soon, in the not too distant future, that personality will also be able to adapt and change to each individual. When it learns from our biometric and psychometric phone data, it's entirely plausible that 'who' we start with, won't be 'who' we end up with.

WE SPEND A VERY LONG TIME MAPPING THE USER JOURNEY AND PLOTTING THE CUSTOMER JOURNEY WHEN IN REALITY, EVERY HUMAN IS ON A JOURNEY WE KNOW NOTHING ABOUT.

The use of virtual assistants such as Alexa, Siri, Cortana and Google Now has all come about due to advances in machine learning and natural language processing, which means that we can frame our enquiries in the sort of language that we use in daily living. We no longer find it strange to seek answers from inanimate helpers – many of our devices, including wearable technology, incorporate this facility – and we don't need to issue standardised commands to get the responses we need. We do need to initiate the help, however, and the futuristic, omnipresent invisible assistant remains the creation of science fiction for now – while the question of allowing a form of autonomy to machines includes weighty considerations such as whether they will act in our best interests and that will always be attributable to us, who we are and our collective psychological condition. To answer these questions relating to power balance and trust, the designer needs extensive knowledge of human-behaviour and this is where the psychologist and data scientist bringing perspective and understanding of Natural Language Processing, is increasingly vital to the emerging design process.

The conversation surrounding human-focused digital products, for me, is about a technically charged world designed deliberately to nourish and understand us rather than distract and replace us. The brilliance of the time and place we live in now, is that technology can now do the things I could only dream about at the start of my career when I was reading Kurzweil. The past twenty years wasn't about getting it wrong; it was about getting **us** ready. We just had to make a lot of mistakes on the way to being prepared. It's been trial and error and errors are good: they help us learn—a lot. My big lesson learnt was that ninety-five percent of the digital vapour we created has been unneeded, and thanks to the power of Artificial Intelligence powered by sophisticated Machine Learning algorithms, we can now look to a digital world with more value to society.

When digital products start to make use of complex sentiment analysis and natural language processing – mood tracking – we turn a corner into a land that is genuinely human-focused. Natural language processing (NLP), in essence, refers to the way technology can derive the meaning out of a human sentence. This process involves near contextual levels of correlation between keywords and referencing through a database to provide only human-like responses. This is the progression, and it's been experimental until now. But, we've just turned a corner.

When you couple Natural Language Processing and Natural Language Understanding, with emotion focused analysis, you start to understand the polarity of someone's personality and self. To do this, a computer makes use of a scaling mechanism, which can rate words based on the happy to sad scale. Advanced methodologies also include subjectivity/objectivity differentiation, and feature-based sentiment analysis. It's a brilliant progression to a more supportive world. The emergence of technology that understands me, rather than technology that just gets in my way. For this to work efficiently, two things must be of absolute importance in the experience – either the person must interact with the technology as honestly as possible, and with no agenda, or the design should be capable of monitoring your organically generated data, from calls, apps and messages, to learn the dynamics of your life (I almost wrote 'the meaning of life' there, which is quite a terrifying thought). There are obvious ethical concerns with the latter, but let us imagine a world where, if even for a moment, we trust things enough to allow them to get to know us. Real-time tracking would help any system become better.

What if your operating system could calculate the time you've spent online chatting? Monitor those chats and efficiently deduce for what percentage of the time you were happy… or annoyed? Let's take things a step further, wherein the operating system could even conclude with whom or what you are most comfortable interacting with, and with whom or what you aren't that eager to engage. What if it could then explain the whys to you? For some, entering a field of study like psychology and reading two hundred books in the dark of the night beside ink-well and paraffin lamp is simply too time-consuming. What if all of that material could live within a body of intelligence that was then able to work *with you*, on *your level* of understanding, to teach you… about yourself. Pure digital enlightenment rather than just digital entitlement?

When I started all those years ago I never once thought that machines would ever replace humans. There will be no 'deus ex machina'—god from the machine—because, frankly, when asked to recall a good experience, most people will remember something that another person did for them, not how a machine worked, and that will never change. My theories of human-focused digital tell us that being human trumps all technological augmentation but designing your technology from the point of view of the human and studying what it means to be human and adding that into everything we design, from physical interfaces to invisible ones powered by words, thoughts and new ways of attaching ourselves to knowledge, is the only sure way of making sure that as the machines continue to evolve, so, in turn, does our humanity. These days, the latest Ai devices can't just gauge our mood from what we say and how we say it: they can work out the best way to respond to cheer you up. All people seek happiness. This is without exception. Whatever different means they employ, they all tend to this end.

The need to uncover moments of happiness in our daily lives has led to us actively seeking small pleasures. Ones that then stimulate an experience to ripple into fleeting moments we call happy. Perhaps if we replace happiness with the word meaningfulness, then we would find ourselves cultivating experiences that can influence our actual well-being, but also that of our broader communities. Observation suggests that the more we interact with screens, the more we are trying to generate the fleeting moment. It seems unlikely we'll discover these pleasures indefinitely, be they transient or long term by interacting with computer screens.

Genuinely harmonious interaction with future technologies will begin once the design of physical interface falls back – and through the medium of voice control and visual communication, we will be free to be us while tech supports our living ways, it having been designed with us as its focus this time around.

If you look at the history of computing, starting with the jacquard loom in 1801, humans have always had to interact with machines in a abstract, complex way. Over time, these methods have become less complex: the punch card gave way to machine code, machine code to the command line, command line to the GUI. But machines still force us to come to them on their terms, speaking their language. The next step is for machines to finally understand us on our own terms, in our own natural words, behaviours, and gestures. Andy Goodman, Fjord

The personalised experience that we can expect for our future selves will be dependent on an interface with visual and auditory capacity so that we can interact, ask questions to and receive responses from. It will be aware of us as individuals due to its ability to match our voice patterns and appearances to a profile it has built and will respond to our requests to carry out a multitude of online tasks. In a significant step forward, it will accomplish these things while adapting to our moods that it recognises through tone of voice and facial expression and using what it knows of our personality to ensure it keeps us happy, while itself being in a constant state of upgrade. Its relationship with us will be proactive in as much as it will refrain from judgement – if that is what you so require. By understanding and caring for our emotional pulse, it is highly adaptive with one mission: service. Consequently, this dynamic helps it reach further into our knowledge basin to also understand what makes us happy or unhappy, wealthy or miserable, trapped or free – and this drive to develop such an intelligence is now necessary as, without an emotional dimension to the construct, technology's ability to serve us further will soon conclude. Etiquette is what it will next come to master, as well as timing, and things we are perhaps even yet unable to comprehend, perhaps even—the nature of the self. This emotional intelligence is the result of storing and analysing only human behaviour over sustained periods that are pinned to the individual it serves. This way it is genius, in a constant state of learning and re-learning. Next, it will know how to make predictions relative to your interests. Yes, for it to leap there and become emotionally aware is a great leap, acting eventually on emotional cues themselves and becoming self-aware. In time, it experiences its own fear, anger, and pleasure. This is an interaction that will serve the person, as it is undergoing those states of being that are relevant to its progress as a piece of continually upgrading intelligence, with every facet of its blueprint built to serve you.

So the answer to our current digital dilemmas is, in fact, all too human. While the past favoured those who could retain and process information efficiently, the future belongs to those who can imagine a better world and work with others to make it happen, and as I stare with an almost panoramic view of my industry and how it reaches into the panorama of our world, I am seeing this future being imagined. There is a lot to look forward to; there is a lot to solve...

My optimistic view of the future is strange to some but when I look back over the last twenty years of digital ups and digital downs, it is a beautiful revolution we started and all those people I've observed glued to monitors on desks and in their hands have played a part in advancing not only our industry but civilisation beyond recognition. I mentioned earlier in the book this idea that perhaps we've all unknowingly played our role in a vast experiment on a scale never attempted and I stand by that. The gifts we were given as humans were in our ability to guess what might lie in front and plot courses toward it. To take gambles intentionally and unintentionally. As a species, we've pursued quite relentlessly as many altruistic goals as evil wrongs. It's the eternal balance, and I can't imagine a world where that ever changes.

So during this vast experiment of the past two decades and the new behaviours and exaggerated mental states we encouraged, we also did something else – we collected enough observational behavioural information to start to learn and therefore stave off the silent killers that lurk amongst society. Hundreds of millions are spent around the world every day to find cures for the diseases that steal our loved ones. Cancer, Alzheimer's, strokes, heart attacks, obesity and smoking. These are the grim reapers. But only a fraction of the money is spent trying to prevent the invisible killers: depression, bipolar, suicide. It's okay – they were never forgotten about, we just couldn't engage in the abstract. But we used the power technology gave us to build behavioural analytics platforms that track browsing behaviour for selling people better products and learning about consumerism. By chance, we also created the technology we needed to teach the silent sufferers and the lonely about themselves. To know thyself. To help thyself. What an exciting opportunity we created.

⌘

If the glass interfaces of today do begin to shrink away and more people start using voice or chat as the primary interface, an Ai could search a transcript and look for those linguistic clues. What's fascinating to me is that the more data an algorithm is 'trained' on, the more confidently and accurately a person's state of mind could be predicted. The possibility of bolstering someone's judgment with a more objective, quantitative data feels like a brave new world. I do believe that this technology we've created could someday help us be more rounded people, and help us live our lives more efficiently. And that could be crucial, given the shortage of mental-health-care providers. If humans aren't going to be the cost-effective solution, we have to leverage tech in some way to extend and augment the physician's reach.

In the technological world, we recently hit an inflexion point that's going to give us a tremendous opportunity to do what I always dreamed we could—help vulnerable people, even before they know they need help. Artificial Intelligence, which has always been the subject of science fiction, is now mature enough to handle some of the most complex challenges. Perhaps even the kinds of human problems that would traditionally require a trained professional. Now, that statement might sound controversial, but I just want to point out that we have to train a machine to learn in much the same way that a human needs to train to be an entirely qualified professional. So we can get a machine on par, if not smarter than a person with any given subject. The real challenge comes with empathy—because that's a trait that only humans can learn—right? To a degree, yes, but because of the sophisticated emotional and sentiment analytics software at our disposal, we can generate dialogues between a human and a machine that is so intelligent and delivered in such an elegant way, that they become almost as good, if not better than the real thing. It's also worth keeping in mind that Artificial Intelligence doesn't sleep, it doesn't eat, it can't make mistakes or have a bad day, and it can service tens, hundreds, thousands, even unlimited numbers of people, simultaneously. We can learn incredible amounts. What a wonderful world.

As computers come to understand those that they serve, the need for a physical interface diminishes. Suddenly, it's not about designing the next technological advance anymore. Instead, we're interacting in a way that's not tied to a single device or location, but we are building a relationship with a machine that learns to understand us and help us know us. To know thyself has been the mission of every culture, bible, philosophical school, existential dream, impressionist's great journey. From Van Gough and Dali to Nietzsche and Hemingway, Jesus and Buddha to Mohammed and Yoda, people have studied the self, at all angles, upside down and inside out. Who am I, what am I? We have asked again and again and again. All tech is going to do is help contribute to the discussion, and in doing so, it will help us realise more about who we are and what we are and what we are not. It will help us access the higher reality that Plato showed we could all reach for if only we are prepared to stand... and leave the cave.

In Plato's *Allegory of The Cave*, we learn of the human condition: prisoners are born into a cave and chained to a wall, and their necks are fixed. As a result, are lacking the knowledge of the world outside the cave. Reality is all they can see. In *Departure From The Cave*, one prisoner becomes free of his cell and experiences the bright light and the immensity of the real world. But he is so overwhelmed that he considers a return, back into the cave. In the allegory, Socrates is asking questions, and the allegory is presented by Plato in *The Republic* to discuss the effect of the lack of education on our nature, on our human condition, on who we are. In the allegory, the prisoners who are born into bondage believe that the shadows they see on the cave are real and the sounds they hear come from the moving shadows, also real—as they are unable to observe any other reality. All that they know is all that they can see, taste, hear, smell and touch, which is limited in their relative world. Once the freed prisoner is taken out of the cave—where the sunbeams and the discomfort of his new reality seem unadjustable... valid questions emerge surrounding our condition and the relationships we have with our changing environments. Soon, the prisoner adapts and can see things for what they are, the water, the sun, the stars and the moon. Then:

"Wouldn't he remember his first home, what passed for wisdom there, and his fellow prisoners... Moreover, were he to return there, wouldn't he be rather bad at their game, no longer being accustomed to the darkness?"

Then: if the prisoner returns to the cave, and tries to free his old friends to show them the light – would they not try to kill him?

"And if they were somehow able to get their hands on and kill the man who attempts to release and lead them up, wouldn't they kill him?"

The darkness of the cave after the freed one has returned signifies the ignorance of the reality that the freed one once existed within. In the allegory, Socrates asks if the remaining prisoners would not try to explain to the freed one that the upward journey has damaged his eyes and other senses and so what he recalls he experienced was not real, and thus, they shall *not* undertake such a trip, for their safety.

Despite the danger of returning to the cave and facing the prisoners that may kill the freed one, it is argued that the freed one should nonetheless, return – despite his now knowing what may become of him and the risk he will face from the other prisoners – because the information that he has *must* be told, spoken, and communicated, despite its dangers.

The freed prisoner is like the philosopher, released from the cave and stepping between worlds, his new reality of adventure and his old home, the great outdoors and the cave. Which direction he goes and when is up to him, and how much time he spends in his different worlds is for no one else to decide. Only him. Only her. Only you. Deep down, when we clear our minds of all of the messages, this is something that we already know. Because it is in the silence where we can feel the answers. From within that silence, we are reaching into the future, it is like a tiny gap that lives between the now and the next bit, and it is there where pure imagination lives and our wonderful creations manifest – and it is there we must bravely go.

The advertising world and consumer society is a symptom of the noise in our minds. If we clear that, the fog in the world will also clear, leaving only the balance and flow we try to find from buying things. How we clear that noise in our minds, I leave to you to explore. I have my ways. You will have yours.

⌘

Throughout my little book, I have tried to explain that understanding the human condition and designing for it will not only be the right move forward, but it is also the trajectory of all emergent technologies anyway because this is the direction nature requires. I know it's not an easy book to read and many of you will not have even reached this page. Or, some of you may just use the odd chapter here and there as quote and reference. That's fine.

Always remember that there is only one of you in the entire universe. You are unique. The chances of you, existing in this room, at this time, as you are 1 in 102,685,000 – zero basically. That's all to do with the chances of your parents' meeting, you being successfully conceived, the cells forming in a certain order, etc. The reason I'm ending my book reminding you of that is that it's critical always to remember that you are brilliant, but technology is not. It's just a dumb enabler and deciding how to make machines that are 'intelligently artificial', will always pale in significance to the fact that it was you that made that magic happen in the first place.

Telling you what the human conditions are and what we are and who we are – this is too much to ask of one person, one designer, who just likes to ask why. And so I put it back to you, because it is the study of the self and who we are and what is right and bad that we all need to embrace – not necessarily the answers to the questions, but merely embracing the journey of the questions. This is our joint responsibility as we build into the future, for the benefit of all beings.

Think. Feel. Build *better* things. Explore. See you in the future. *That's why.*

ACKNOWLEDGEMENTS

A book like this doesn't get written without the wisdom and support of many, many brilliant thinkers and a career like mine doesn't take flight without the guidance of the wisest and most kind.

A massive debt of gratitude to **Mr Luke Shipman**: my editor and collaborator. When I approached Luke it was meant to be just to take my unstructured thoughts, numerous disparate articles, keynotes and ramblings and help shape them into a book. We grabbed snippets of time together, throughout the year, discussing my design philosophies, swapping emails, exchanging Evernote messages and numerous SMS messages at all hours. What emerged was a true collaboration. This book would never have happened without his patience.

A big shout out to **Dan Thwaites** for being my counsel and mentor for well over fifteen years. There's always a voice of reason whenever I need it and that's invaluable when you're a character like me. Someone who doesn't naturally conform and often upsets the status quo.

Twenty years ago, a man called **Stuart Lee** fished a rough fifteen-year-old out of school and took a huge gamble, giving him a job in his digital design department at a helicopter factory. That *boy* will be forever grateful to you. That kindness also pays forward in the young, energetic teenagers I meet today.

All the wonderful designers – how on earth can I find the words to say thank you to the incredible talent I've been influenced by over the years? All the many, many designers who worked for me and followed my lead (even often against the grain and against the party line). What an astonishing group of people you are. Without you, the world would stay in one place. You inspire me every single day. There are too many of you to name, but needless to say you are all ingrained in some way within this book.

ABOUT THE AUTHOR

Pete Trainor

Pete is a husband, father, digital designer, public speaker, accidental polymath and co-founder of US Ai in London. He speaks all over the world about Design, Artificial Intelligence, Creative and Social Technologies and the physiological and psychological effects on their audiences. Pete regularly appears in UK and international press as an analyst on digital media, creative industries, emergent technologies, and tech markets.

Over the last decade, Pete has helped to pioneer an entirely new approach to Ai focused products and services, one that looks at 'self-evolving systems' and 'minimum viable personality' to help solve societal and human issues.

His service design and technology business, Us Ai, is one of the U.Ks leading companies in the field of 'Applied Ai'. They create custom, data powered solutions to solve and automate a range of human focused challenges, from chat based interactions, to bulk task automation and machine learning.

A vocal mental health campaigner, he calls for better use of technology to help men, women, children and teens in moments of crisis.

He has a very simple mantra: Don't do things better, do *better* things.

You can follow Pete on Twitter: @petetrainor

If you found this book useful, inspiring, enlightening and all the things in-between, please tweet about it using the tag **#hippobook** and remember to share this copy with other people.